A Failed System

A Failed System

Pandemic-Related Solutions to a 200-Year-Old Education Crisis

Eldon "Cap" Lee

ROWMAN & LITTLEFIELD
Lanham • Boulder • New York • London

Published by Rowman & Littlefield
An imprint of The Rowman & Littlefield Publishing Group, Inc.
4501 Forbes Boulevard, Suite 200, Lanham, Maryland 20706
www.rowman.com

86-90 Paul Street, London EC2A 4NE, United Kingdom

Copyright © 2022 by Eldon "Cap" Lee

All rights reserved. No part of this book may be reproduced in any form or by any electronic or mechanical means, including information storage and retrieval systems, without written permission from the publisher, except by a reviewer who may quote passages in a review.

British Library Cataloguing in Publication Information Available

Library of Congress Cataloging-in-Publication Data

Names: Lee, Eldon, 1942– author.
Title: A failed system : pandemic-related solutions to a 200-year-old education crisis / Eldon "Cap" Lee.
Description: Lanham, Maryland : Rowman & Littlefield, 2022 | Includes bibliographical references and index. | Summary: "A Failed System is designed to bring the current system of education out of the dark ages by way of a new structure that puts students on an even playing field. The solutions offered entail a new system and philosophy of education along with a curriculum that takes students beyond the classroom onto their pathway to success"—Provided by publisher.
Identifiers: LCCN 2022006434 (print) | LCCN 2022006435 (ebook) | ISBN 9781475865981 (paper) | ISBN 9781475865998 (epub)
Subjects: LCSH: Educational change—United States. | Education—Aims and objectives–United States. | School improvement programs—United States. | Motivation in education.
Classification: LCC LA217.2 .L434 2022 (print) | LA217.2 (ebook) | DDC 370.973/370.973—dc23
LC record available at https://lccn.loc.gov/2022006434
LC ebook record available at https://lccn.loc.gov/2022006435

To Victoria C. Lee, my beautiful daughter

Remembering Carita Lee, Mike Heckathorn, and others who left us too soon

Contents

Foreword ix

Preface xi

Acknowledgments xiii

Chapter 1: Exposing the Catastrophic Past 1

Chapter 2: Developing a Pathway to Success 15

Chapter 3: Eluding the Failed Policies of the Past 31

Chapter 4: Exploring the World beyond the Classroom 51

Chapter 5: Quashing the Testing Obsession 73

Chapter 6: Straight Talk 93

Chapter 7: Help Is on the Way 111

Bibliography 127

Index 129

About the Author 131

Foreword

A product of 53206, the much-maligned Milwaukee, Wisconsin, zip code, as an undergraduate student in a social work practicum, I visited a young client's school. The Milwaukee Village School, followed a new school model. As a school within a school, I entered the doors of my high school alma mater, was buzzed upstairs, and was met with a community of "we." Immediately, it was clear that the folks at the Village embraced wrap-around services and were actively engaged in delivering education to the whole child.

Amongst those folks, a tall, shaggy-haired man emerges from The Village Square. The suit, keys, and the walkie were weights that marked him as the administrative leader. I have gone on from that day in 1995 as a social work student to seasoned educator status. My first years at the Milwaukee Village were under his tutelage and leadership. My first principal is noted as an authentic leader, Eldon "Cap" Lee—a brilliant mind. Lee has the heart of an activist. I would say, "He is most comfortable, I believe, without props and accessories." I am forever grateful to have crossed his path.

His purpose is precise and clear: Give children what they need and educate them. I found that to be a rarity. Children are people with minds and hearts that are developing and deserving of better than the status quo. I appreciate this as his message and mission. It made working for others, later, a challenge. Some of the most important lessons I have learned were taught through the opportunities extended during my time at the Village. These have proven invaluable over the years. As a high schooler in zip code 53206, the first lesson for me was reaffirm rather than profile by zip codes.

As presented in this book, educators take alternative measures to assess student needs, building on their strengths and their individual interests. Unheard of at that time, teachers were encouraged to expose the child to something new and teach them how to face that challenge while *maximizing* their potential. A community gardening project or a construction group that has fluidity in its learning environment were welcomed activities. I could teach the 3R's and social skills seamlessly, in the building, at the construction site, or in the farmer's market.

With COVID-19 the light has shone. The pandemic has been nature's way of revealing over two hundred years of pre-existing inequalities in society exacerbated in our education system. Yes, in this book, Mr. Lee is pointing to systemic failure in public schools' inability to educate all children. This book highlights brainwashing in preparation for standardized tests, and memorization and regurgitation of information that stands as rhetoric of politicians and large corporate entities while widening racial and economic inequalities.

The lens Mr. Lee portrays is making pointed observations about schools living through one initiative after another. Whether Goals 2000, Common Core, or Race to The Top, he is honest with the reader. Somewhere public education lost its way and still has not gotten to the core or to the top. Mr. Lee is an authentic activist and educational reformist. I endear his "I told you so" is not merely anecdotal because I know The Village School was tried by fire and we as a team walked the walk. That project presented a succinct alternative. This book offers a healing balm and manifest for serving children as unique individuals. It works; I have seen it.

—Dr. LaShawn Roscoe Scott, teacher

Preface

The system of education, as it existed in the late eighteenth century, had its purpose described by Thomas Jefferson as "raking a few geniuses from the rubbish." Jefferson, however, wanted education to be available to poor as well as rich people and worked toward that goal. The reality is that ranking and sorting students was a mainstay during those years. This practice was one that survived throughout the centuries and exists today.

With that in mind, an innovative school was started within the Milwaukee Public Schools that was allowed to take a new way of thinking into the realm of education. Upon observing the destructive policies of the past, and my experiences of designing and implementing that Milwaukee Village School, I realized that the type of innovation needed would not be able to co-exist with the current system of education. I retired and began writing immediately. It was time to stop raking a few geniuses from the rubbish, especially since, in the eyes of the eighteenth-century elite, some didn't even rise to the level of rubbish.

Enter the coronavirus crisis. The amount of time students were confined to their homes, away from in-school learning, was devastating to their education. For those who had no access to computers as well as those whose learning styles were not suitable for computer learning, now had their future shaken to the core. It soon became clear that with skill levels now all over the board, those students would not return to school fitting into the "one size fits all" education currently available.

What grade are they in? Were they passed with their age group without learning? Were they retained, allowing the "raking" process to begin? Or were they given sitting time in summer school also allowing them to proceed without learning? The lessons from the pandemic were clear. Not only does the system not work for them anymore, the system hasn't worked for some students for the last 200 years.

In the last four books I authored and co-authored I hit on the same issues. But now, reality strikes home to many. For decades if not centuries, Black and

Brown students have been ignored by the education elite. While the geniuses got raked upward, those children who elite politicians found easy to ignore were often pushed into the school-to-prison pipeline or into the streets like rubbish. This must never happen again. The misfortune of the coronavirus crisis, as devastating as it was, opened the eyes of many who remained silent throughout the years.

After experiencing five years creating and implementing an innovative school, it became clear that the current system of education was never designed to serve all children. That these schools and this system cannot be fixed—it must be replaced. Herein describes detailed ideas on how to replace that failed system of education as well as explanations as to why it must be fixed. The question from the coronavirus crisis that looms heavy in our minds is "what grade do students really belong in, are they passed without learning, or retained into oblivion"? That question is one of many that is answered in this book.

There are no solutions under the current system of education! But don't give up hope. This book is full of solutions!

Acknowledgments

Mary Gale Budzisz whose words show up everywhere in this book.
Victoria Lee for her assistance.
Luz Estela Narvaez Lambrano for her ongoing support.
Steven Narvaez and Luis Vargas for technical support.
Every student and athlete with whom I had the pleasure of sharing education.

Chapter 1

Exposing the Catastrophic Past

Albert Einstein said, "in the midst of every crisis, lies great opportunity." This phrase could never be more appropriate than to describe the effort needed to serve today's students. The effects of the coronavirus crisis struck a blow that reached out to every student in every corner of the globe. There is no one on earth who has not been affected by this deadly disease. Bustling cities have become ghost towns. Stores, restaurants, sporting events, and more have closed. However, they do not come close to the impact of schools shutting down denying so many children of an education.

The hope was that this virus would dissipate within a few short weeks. However, as those short weeks turned into months it became clear that teachers must find a way to educate students in their homes. Enter technology. FaceTime, Zoom, and Skype are now seen as the saviors of education in this crisis. There appear to be no other reasonable choices that will maintain safety and give, at least, a minimal amount of education.

As students return to school with their skills all over the board, one must question whether this has been the case, fully ignored, for the past 200 years.

DEFINING THE PROBLEM

In an effort to save students from more than a year without in-school learning, every creative bone in the body of educators is pushed to the extreme. Technology seems to be the only answer available. It is better than nothing, and nothing is what the students were getting as they were first confined to their homes. How do we reach students scattered across the city, villages, and the countryside? Does everyone even have access to the internet?

IT IS TIME TO PUNT!

Using sports as an analogy, when everything else fails and it is fourth down and thirty yards to go, they punt. Schools are clearly in the same predicament. As time marched on, educators could see that their new-found, technology-driven education would be in it for the long haul. Predictions were that schools would be affected for more than a year. Educators would turn on their after burners and full speed ahead to develop and perfect ways to educate children (hopefully) sitting in front of their computer screens. This is a monumental task diminished more by succumbing to the teach-to-the-test curriculum.

The first challenge is to assure all students are participating in the lessons. This is easier said than done. Those parents who are home from work due to the crisis can guide their children in their daily activities. This is their time to get an understanding of how hard teachers work. But we must remember, most parents are not teachers and have no experience in the rigors required of today's teachers.

For those parents who are not home, working two or three jobs to survive, the children are on the honor system to continue their education. Fortunately, many will continue to do their classwork online. However, many will not. Those children who "need us the most" could easily get lost along the way and retreat to a warm comfortable bed or leave their house for more exciting activities.

What about those who do not have a computer or those whose electricity is turned off due to nonpayments. Or those who do not have access to internet, or even worse, those who have poor connections to the internet. The list goes on and on. Educators are having a real-time experience fretting about how their students are responding as they return to school. Teaching just became more difficult under the current system of education.

These are unique times that require unique responses to education. For a full year, students have been through hell. In addition to missing in-school time, this was the most stressful time of their young lives. They are stuck at home with no activities beyond computer classes and games. Many have been dependent on a decent meal in school while others are completely stressed out and often scared about catching the virus and dying or passing it on to their parents and grandparents.

For those who feel they can educate all children in the same manner, this is a wakeup call of the century. Be ready for a reality check when you realize student's skills were all over the board even before they left for this "virus vacation." Now, upon returning to school, the differences were magnified. One thing is for certain. We cannot go back to a system that was never designed to serve all children.

OBSTACLES TO LEARNING

Secretary of Education Miguel Cardona understands the failures of the past. In a speech he said: "If we think we are going back to how business is done, before the pandemic, then we are missing an opportunity." He also said we must "address inequities that existed long before COVID-19." Let us clearly understand what Secretary Cardona is saying. As we look at the pandemic through a microscope, we find that many students had learning stagnated due to school time missed as well as the stress that goes with such a deadly disease. No longer do they fit the "one size fits all" philosophy of the current system of education.

The truth be known, as we take that same microscope and look at the last 200 years, primarily Black and Brown students as well as some poor White students were often pushed out of school for not fitting in. That is if they were allowed in school at all. The stress put upon these students was well beyond what we see today. Throughout history one size has never fit all.

Here is a fact that educators must consider. Childhood stress literally slows the learning process. Malnutrition, the lack of sleep, poor physical and mental health, and a wide range of other obstacles also affect learning. These are not excuses, these are real. These obstacles have always been there for some children, however, they are now magnified by the extremes caused by the coronavirus crisis.

Following the systemic structure of yesterday, today's education system continues to rank and sort students. Those who score best will thrive while the rest are chosen by an outdated system skewed to assure they are permanently left behind. There are those who continue to believe that all children will perform in the same way and in the same time frames thus becoming the Stepford kids.

The movie from years past called *The Stepford Wives*, showed all families living in the newly formed suburbs of the 50s all acting and talking the same. It is impossible to believe that anyone who would have laughed at that movie for its sarcastic humor, would even think that having all students perform in the same way at the same time could be a goal of education. However, when talking about education, many politicians today want to transport us back to the dreams of 60 years ago.

A reminder that those "dreams" or better yet, "nightmares" of 60 years ago did not include the vast majority of people. Notably absent were, yes, you guessed it, Black and Brown folks as well as some poor White folks. Exclusivity was the norm back then and exclusivity is the norm now. The only difference is, today it is subtle, at least until the coronavirus crisis came along and evened the playing field. Now a wide variety of children are left behind with learning slowed by the stress put on them these past years. We continue the discussion of stress and its effect on learning.

According to Dr. Kara Fitzgerald in her interview on the program "Gene Whispering" with Dr. Moshe Szyf (www.drkarafitzgerald.com, February 27, 2017) she stated:

> So essentially what we saw that a stressful environment really coordinates three kinds of responses in the body: an immune response, a metabolic response, and a behavioral response. And if you remember my talk, I talked about the fact that you cannot break psychiatry from physical health. They are coordinated.
>
> When something stressful or threatening happens, it is not just our brain that is involved. We must recruit everything from the immune system the fat system, to the heart. And therefore, what I believe is early in life, children are getting this information, life is going to be tough. And they are kind of altering multiple systems to deal with hard life. And hard life involves social threat, it involves food threat, lack of food. It involves bacterial infestation, so it prepares for all of this.

Stress is not the only roadblock to learning. According to many studies, your cognitive function, attention span, and capacity to learn and think creatively all suffer when you trade sleep or rest for work. With the loss of sleep, you are losing out on health and poor health has a negative impact on learning. Add to that malnutrition, exposure to lead, and many other issues that impact learning.

For those who do not believe roadblocks affect learning and want to stick to the simplistic policy of science denial, there are many politicians, educators, and naysayers wanting to believe your thoughts. But if you listen to science, along with a truckload of common sense, roadblocks to learning affect children's progress! The reality is while some children in poverty have a clear path to learning, others have devastating roadblocks like childhood stress that slow the learning process.

THE PATH OF SYSTEMIC RACISM

Systemic racism is embedded in schools so deeply that it is hardly noticeable to the trained eye of educators and parents alike. It is this current system of education that drives many students to drop out of school and often pushes them into the school-to-prison pipeline. Recognize that students are pushed out of school more than they drop out. Let us look at systemic racism. This does not mean all educators are racists. However, it means that the entrenched system allows and in some cases forces racism to exist. For years, decades, and even centuries, politicians have turned a blind eye to embedded discrimination.

As we realize the effects of the aforementioned mentioned obstacles to learning, it is time to look at who is affected the most. Clearly in urban areas Black children are the most affected. The availability of guns is one issue that has led to high stress. Imagine a soldier sent on a mission where they lose several buddies in battle. They then return to the barracks to take a standardized test. Add stress to low expectations for those in certain zip codes and the problem becomes clear, albeit more complex.

From the base of a broken system of failure comes a wide range of systemic issues that forces the racial divide to grow. The dominoes begin to fall as one concept is piled upon another to maintain a failed system of education. The systemic destruction begins with the facade that grade levels are an indicator of academic achievement. As evidenced by a wide range of student skills in every grade level, they are not and have never been a true indicator of achievement. Yet the students are all taught as one.

Once children are retained, combined with the zip code expectations, they begin to lose hope for their future. On the second retention for a full school year or a class on the high school level, they begin to realize they will not graduate until they are 20 years old. This realization comes during their freshman year of high school. As they turn 16 years old, they are systematically pushed out of school. This hits hardest on those affected by the devastating roadblocks previously mentioned, Black students imprisoned by a stressful neighborhood and low expectations. These are the problems but what are the solutions?

Consider the rise in earning power of Black and Brown students when we reduce or eliminate the large numbers of students who are "pushed" out of school by a broken system of education. Now is the perfect opportunity for educators to prepare for the wide variety of skills students possess. This means design a system that truly respects the intelligence and abilities of all children. The time has come to realize all children are different, they learn at different rates, in different ways, with different background knowledge, and different experiences. This was exaggerated by the loss of in-school learning during the aforementioned mentioned crisis. Detailed solutions are everywhere in this book.

WHAT GRADE ARE THEY REALLY IN?

Herein lies the dilemma as schools seek solutions to the myriad of problems resulting from the coronavirus crisis: Carolyn Thompson of the Associated Press authored an article in December of 2020 entitled "Schools Confront Off the Rail Numbers of Failing Grades." Here students are failing through no fault of their own. Due to closed schools and the narrow scope of computer learning, they have been denied a complete education. The question arises, will those students be retained? If not, will they actually improve their skills enough to catch up? Or will educators just close their eyes and pretend they increased their level of skills?

Some of the answers to those questions appear in another article by Alejandra O'Conell—Domenech on October 2020 for AMNY: "New York City students will not receive 'F' letter grades under new city grading policy." Facing the other extreme, it appears that New York City will not fail anyone. New York City seems ready to advance students regardless of achievement. Be aware as they use sitting time in summer school as their solution. Do not let them use that age-old trick. Sitting time is never automatically learning time.

What do we do now? Are we really ready for this? Damage begins when a child fails a course or does not learn to the same standard at the same time as others. The system then fails them and retains them in the same grade knowing that every retention leads to a delayed graduation age? Yet another option in dealing with a failing student is to pass them without learning, leaving them to flounder in upper grades as well as when they enter today's society.

Many students will show that learning has stagnated during the coronavirus crisis. Now they either receive failing grades and are being retained or have all "F" grades dismissed and are moving forward without learning. Be prepared for an array of fake solutions to a problem that will not be fixed under the current system of education. Oodles of tutors are brought into schools to give the impression of an effort by school boards to serve struggling students. Not only do many students have to make up for the time they lost, but how many were behind in the first place, passing with a D?

The result is a school system in chaos. There is no reasonable solution to these problems under the current system! A new systemic structure must offer better choices. What are the choices when dealing with a diverse population of students? We may no longer assume that those in certain zip codes, or of a certain race or gender or any other group subject to stereotypical beliefs are all the same. As educators we may no longer assume anything.

This coronavirus crisis has put a magnifying glass on every flaw in the system of education. When students returned to "in-school" learning, did we know what grade to place them in? Most educators are aware that children are not all the same but here is a much-needed wakeup call. With the combination of missing in-school time for reasons aforementioned mentioned and the roadblocks interfering with learning, their skills are scattered all over the board. It is extremely important to understand that as students enter the classroom, educators have no idea whether a child is affected by obstacles or not. So what grade are they in?

Assigning students to a grade level is an impossible task. There is no solution under the current system of education.

The coronavirus crisis delivered a serious blow to student education across the country, not to mention around the world. It did, however, open our eyes to realities that have been evading us for decades. Although exaggerated by the pandemic, most of the roadblocks mentioned have wreaked havoc on our students for decades. The damage is exasperated by a system and philosophy of education that has done little to alleviate the problem.

Consider this, we have students who are severely cognitively disabled, across the spectrum to those we call geniuses, who belong to the Mensa society and belong in college when they are twelve years old. Recently two children, Amber Sunshine, four years old and her brother Brian, age five were found to have IQs in the range of 140–150. These are the extremes. Think of the range of all the students in between. How could anyone believe that all seventh graders have only seventh-grade skills? What grade should they be placed in?

INDIVIDUALIZING EXPECTATIONS

There are those who point to the obstacles in the way of learning and blame poverty and zip codes as the problem. Others say that many in poverty will succeed in this eighteenth-century system if we have high expectations and wish them to a higher level. Of course, high expectations are essential to success but now we must determine how they are defined in the world of individual differences.

If we have high expectations will that severely cognitively disabled student be able to write a doctoral thesis on astrophysics? Not yet. But we must have high expectations for everyone with no limit on how far they can progress. The lack of sufficiently high expectations is a major part of the systemic puzzle. However, these goals will be met one step at a time, not in one giant leap.

Worse is when we celebrate students with straight "A's." That is a perfect example of low expectations. How do we know if they could not do better? Anyone with straight "A's" has not been challenged. The best way to determine if someone is challenged is to take them to a level where they fail, learn from, and overcome that failure pushing their skill level even higher. Often these are the students who did their activities at home during the virus and drift into their straight "A" education without missing a beat. The learning gap widens dramatically.

> Our mechanical, industrialized civilization is concerned with averages, with percent's. The mental habit which reflects this social scene subordinate's education and social arrangements based on averaged gross inferiorities and superiorities.—John Dewey, 1922

Remember the saying "poverty isn't destiny?" Now the conversation is about zip codes. This is another way of using poverty, but this time, by generalizing, it is using poverty as an excuse. Can we tell who is failing by the zip code they are in? Some say zip codes in poor neighborhoods are all in poverty and it is next to impossible for them to succeed. Poverty is not destiny for some and is destiny for others, especially under this current system. And some in zip codes in poor neighborhoods are affected by poverty and others might easily get their PhD or MD.

Those children in poverty that have been sheltered from the obstacles to learning will do well. It is the effects of poverty that are of concern. Many children in poverty have childhood stress and other issues that, under the current eighteenth-century system of education is destiny. The ranking and sorting of students to determine who goes to college on one end of the spectrum and who is forced into the school-to-prison pipeline on the other side must end! That is difficult to do because it has been entrenched for centuries.

Thomas Jefferson referred to education when he said the purpose was to "rake a few geniuses from the rubbish." In their eyes, some did not rise to the level of rubbish. Education is not a game! Education is not running a race! For centuries we have been expecting the "geniuses" to go to college and the rest thrown into the street like "rubbish." This system exists to this day.

WHAT IS ACHIEVEMENT?

Now that students have returned from the "coronavirus crisis," the system must be fixed to get rid of false indicators of academic achievement, no matter who the scores favor. Teachers of kindred minds must stay on message acknowledging that a higher level "whole child" learning is the goal. Now comes the details, all supported by facts, not by generalized beliefs that politicians and educators have followed for years.

> When achievement is restricted to grades, (test scores) attendance, and behavioral compliance, the robust nature of learning is inadvertently restricted . . . traditional school outcomes as level "B" achievement can occur in the absence of learning how to work and learn independently; ("A" level learning includes) learning how to synthesize, transfer and apply knowledge to the world beyond the classroom; learning how to

value self as subjects and not as objects; and learning how to engage in and share power in democratic spaces.—Dr. Angela Dye

Is that not what we want for our children, a first-class education? Today in our high-stakes world of education, we prepare our first graders to be good second graders; our seventh graders to be better eighth graders and our seniors to be better college freshmen. Then, when they receive their PhD, they can get a job and start "A"-level learning from the beginning because it has been absent from the curriculum.

As we rearrange the curriculum to meet the needs of students who have returned from the coronavirus crisis, it is time to consider focusing on the true needs of the students. The kind of needs that help them outside the classroom walls, that they can carry with them through life. That is unlikely to happen in front of a computer screen, at home. That does not happen by a curriculum driven by a standardized test.

If we did not understand that before the pandemic, we certainly will know that now that the students have returned. We must develop a system and philosophy of education that truly does respect the intelligence and abilities of all children. A system that takes students from where they are to a place that will serve them well. That will prepare every child for their future with level "A" achievement. No longer may education be a race to see who goes to college and who is thrown into the school-to-prison pipeline. Understand that children do not drop out of school, they get pushed out and that is unthinkable.

American Federation of Teachers president Randi Weingarten said in a speech: "We must do far more than physically return to schools, as important as that is to create the normalcy we crave. We also need to recover and reimagine with an eye to a renaissance in public education." And we must: "Encourage Education Secretary Miguel Cardona to form a task force to rethink how we assess student learning and how to measure what really counts."

MEASURE WHAT REALLY COUNTS

Secretary Cardona has said we must: "address inequities that existed long before COVID-19." Will we, as an education community, now realize the enormity of the task before us. Looking back at the conflict over what grades students should receive for the work they did at home we must ask the question, what are we assessing? Are we assessing what really counts or are we assessing for convenience?

I refer to Dr. Dye's comments. "When achievement is restricted to grades, (test scores) attendance, and behavioral compliance, the robust nature of learning is inadvertently restricted." Is it no wonder educators do not know what grades to give those students who returned from the coronavirus crisis? This conflict has existed for years. If we average test scores and add in behavior reports and attendance, what is it that we are assessing?

At Milwaukee Village School, small pretests were given to determine a jumping off point for the child's education. A parent came in as we informed her that her seventh grade son was reading on the level of a fourth grader. We then indicated what we would do to improve that skill. The parent was livid. She said at his last school her son got a "C" in reading so he must be average, on level.

Letter grades say absolutely nothing about a child's skills. The other school lied and deceived that parent into believing a "C" grade really meant average. When one educator was asked what letter grades meant, the facetious response was "A" means good, "B" means kind of good, "C" means average even though no one can say what average is as it differs from class to class. "D" means kind of dumb, and "F" means . . . you get the idea.

The concept of grades goes back over one hundred years. What the coronavirus crisis taught us was there are no legitimate grades we can give students. How can a total school's grade point average be 2.0 during this pandemic when so many "F's" were given? Isn't 2.0 supposed to mean average for the school? Or is it for the city, or state, or country. Does anyone know? The problem is easily resolved. Simply do not give "F's" like the New York Schools and pretend everyone has learned.

LOOKING BACK

The challenge ahead begins with looking back at all the reforms presented as the solution to the ills of education. As painful as it is, moving forward can only happen when the past is reviewed with a critical eye. How do we reform the reform that has never worked? Innovation is not consistent with "best practices" because "best practices" are based on what has been tried. Innovation is based on what has never been tried.

THE HISTORY OF REFORM

Suffering through the coronavirus crisis shined the light on the failures of the past. Education reform has attempted to make radical change to education while ignoring the one change that would put every child on an even playing field. Combining all the problems magnified by the coronavirus crisis along with all the attempts at reform leads to only one logical conclusion, the system of education is broken.

Beginning with "Goals 2000," the standardizing of education was off to a conspicuous start. Their goals expected all children to reach competency in reading and math at the fourth, eighth, and twelfth grade level. Needless to say, by the year 2000, that goal was not reached. It did, however, begin a journey down a path that was to lead to a culture of failure for students and educators alike.

Following Goals 2000, The No Child Left Behind Act was designed to improve on past failures. Again, this was a devastating failure, and it did damage to so many children. That bill had the false expectation that every child could be at the same place at the same time on their test-driven proficiency. Maintaining the same belief that test scores were actually indicators of achievement, they were attempting the impossible.

However, there is a minuscule of information that was important to the movement toward quality education for all. It was the first time that we, as a nation, started considering the importance of every child. Think about it, our education philosophy has never concerned itself with those who moved slower through the system or those who moved faster. This is a small step, but an important one in the process of whole child education reform.

Another formula was then attempted. Common Core utilized a failed top-down concept that subtly developed guidelines from the federal and the state level to impose on all children. Again, it was test-driven thus lending itself to yet another level of failure. As test scores came in all over the board, one would wonder if they could ever succeed at getting every child to proficiency at the same time. However, the agenda-driven politicians were adamant that only if given more sitting time and developing a little more grit, they would succeed. That did not happen.

Common Core forced educators to look at a proficiency system of education. Letter grades and grade levels would no longer be recognized as the only indicators of a student's achievements. Common Core forced educators to focus on, what they considered was actual learning of each individual child. Unfortunately, not only did that use a narrow scope of the standardized test, but they then took that information to treat all children as an extension of one person leading to yet another failure and the need to move on.

A stretch of the imagination would have RTTT, The Race to The Top, as a step forward. In this race, states were awarded points for various policies that were thought to improve innovation in education. The goal was to turn around low-performing schools. Of course, the failure was to base a school's success on the high-stakes standardized test with minimal recognition of the student's differences in those schools. Read carefully and repeat after me, children do not start the race from the same place!

With competition at its base, students were forced into a win-lose situation on schools that drove them away from the fundamental purpose of education. Winning became more important than learning. Failing at this led to the discovery of what not to do with the system of education. It is amazing that everyone wants better schools but few, if any, want different schools.

When discussing systemic change, the response is often that those who want innovation are simply ideologues. After all, they say, we went to school back in the day and we turned out alright. That issue is debatable. Let it be known that the dreamers are the ones who ignite the flame of progress. Given that systemic change, as difficult as it will be, is about the only reform that has not been tried. When all else fails, look to the dreamers. And all else has failed.

DEMOLISHING THE JOY OF LEARNING

There is no rule that indicates rigor, grit, and other contrived catchwords are not allowed to relate to that joy. It is, however, the policy of the past. Hard work is not analogous to drudgery. Hard work, when it is a work of passion will incorporate rigor and grit. As success is defined by the standardized test, the whole philosophy of education is designed to an artificial goal thus taking every ounce of joy out of the process of learning.

"Teach to the test" then touches benchmarks, the daily schedule, and class times while eliminating the arts, shop class, home economics, and just about anything else that teaches to the world beyond the classroom. The immediate goal is to teach to the whole child as well as to restore the passion for learning that drives the student on their pathway to success. The pathway to success does not lead to a standardized test.

Understand that the joy of learning does not mean play, or simply running around having fun. It also does not mean turning lessons into play time although that is the way it will be described by the naysayers. It means the joy of accomplishment, working toward the goal of a successful future. A child does not have to be miserable to display rigor or grit. Does Giannis Antetokounmpo lack rigor or grit when working out or playing basketball? Not at all. And judging from his smile after winning the NBA championship, my suspicion is that he has plenty of joy in his job.

What about Yo-Yo Ma or Mikhail Baryshnikov or Serena Williams? Of course, there are times when they have pain and stress, but without the joy their success would be diminished. The will to succeed is a joyful experience. It is essential to remember that children will memorize when we tell them only to be left with little true knowledge. That is what the past has to offer. However, the reality is, students will learn when they are ready. Children still control their minds and will open or close them based on their perception of the value of the incoming information. The joy of learning opens many minds driving the children on their pathway to success.

The joy of discovery means empowering children to work together to research, analyze, debate, and draw conclusions in a way that is real. How better to learn about farming than to visit a farmer and put their hands in the soil. Learning about being an engineer is an exciting adventure when students can talk to and watch them do their job. Rigor and grit can be demonstrated best when students are engulfed in their passions.

The love of music is inherent in many children. Why not use it as an outlet for rigor? Music is a valuable communication tool and plays a major role in the history of the world, yet it is diminished in our school system. Add to that dance, comedy, graphic design, photography, fashion design, culinary arts, game design while incorporating reading writing math, and other academic necessities in them. It is easy to do.

For those rigor and grit experts who salivate at the thought of eliminating recess, consider this. Not only would children lose exercise, so important to the brain and body, but they have also lost a respite from the classroom and time in which children used their imaginations to fill their day with joy and creativity. Watch them use their skills to invent games like many of us did years ago. What a great learning experience. As drudgery increases in schools, so does the failure and dropout rates. Imagine how the arts could be built into every academic area to make learning real.

No longer can we as teachers look into the eyes of students the system has failed and see hopelessness.

LOOKING FORWARD

In the pages ahead, we will develop a system where standards are guidelines for success rather than deadlines for failure. Where every child has a vision for the future. This will not be easy, but it will be worth it. Ahead we will discuss ways to take students out of the race to be first onto a system of education that puts a focus on learning, starting wherever the student skills lay at that particular time.

As we change the way we look at the educational process, we must also change the way we assess schools. By giving a clear assessment of a school, we will stop the practice of prejudging those who serve the students who need us the most. No longer may we look at average standardized test scores and judge a school. We expect schools to make individual student progress toward their goals.

Education is to prepare all students for the world outside the classroom. Always remember that obstacles to learning are only one piece of the puzzle. There are many other concerns that will keep a people down. This discussion is focused on the system and philosophy of education. "Those who do not remember the past, are bound to repeat it."—Spanish philosopher George Santayana. Not only will we remember the past, we will expose it for the damage it has done to children.

> We are still trying to develop both the philosophy as well as the system of education which really does respect the intelligence and abilities of ordinary people.—James Anderson

Chapter 2

Developing a Pathway to Success

Fundamental to developing a new systemic design is to gather information that will bring a stronger focus to student needs. No longer may we throw out education for students to catch in a bushel basket. From the experience of the coronavirus crisis, we realize that student's skills and abilities will be scattered all over the board. The possibility of a "one size fits all" approach to education must no longer exist. We must also recognize that it will be extremely difficult to provide 1200 different plans for 1200 students in a school. That would be a nightmare.

What we can do, however, is utilize creative groupings to assure all students are on their pathway to success. With creative groupings, differentiated instruction, a cautious use of technology, community experiences as well as a variety of other creative teaching methods, every child will be assured of getting an appropriate education. Of course, this will require small class sizes as well as sufficient planning time to meet the needs of all children.

IMPLEMENTING THE MAP

There is no shortcut to providing a quality education for all. No longer may we be comfortable throwing students into the school-to-prison pipeline for the sole purpose of saving money. The consequences are a much higher cost in the future, not only for more prisons, but for more police and more social programs. In addition, lower employment levels decrease the tax base leading to a tremendous loss for the economy.

FORMULATING A BASE LINE

As the MAP to the future is developed, a baseline, or "jumping off point," will allow for a basic understanding of student abilities. From this baseline the MAP to the future is developed. It will be exciting for the student to check off learning goals as they are achieved and compare them to their baseline. This can be done at all levels, elementary, middle, and high school. Here are some thoughts as teachers prepare for their new educational adventure:

- Gather student information: To begin, educators must make every effort to gather information about every student. This includes class assessments, school projects, and any other information that gives insight into the learning level of the student. This does not mean grades or grade point averages, attendance records, behavior reports, and so forth.

  This means actual educational information. Some testing information may help. It may be difficult to retrieve information from previous years. If so, start classroom assessments as soon as possible. There is no time to waste, especially not the four months it takes information from the high stakes standardized test to arrive. Remember, the assessment information goes directly to the teacher for immediate use.
- Small pretest: During the students' first month in school, a small pretest, one-on-one, will be given for reading and math. Although time consuming, it is essential to get the best information possible and students have a clear understanding of the issues. One way to tackle this problem of one-on-one is to free up any educator, who is not assigned a class, to give this test. Included could easily be retired teachers. A simple pretest is easy to give and will be passed to the teacher at once.
- Compare information: The teacher will then compare that test information with the child's classwork to assure accuracy and a "jumping off point" for learning. Many of these tests are already given. The difference is, along with classroom assessments, there will be no need for the high stakes standardized test. They will be used immediately. And they will be given one-on-one to assure accurate results.
- All subject areas, other than math and reading, should be assessed, however not by a written test. Develop a demonstration of learning that will help teachers plan for the student's future. A good example is a science project. Is it not better to demonstrate the scientific method rather than memorizing it? Assessments are inclusive of all subject areas. As a guide, teachers can take note on how science fairs, band and orchestra competitions, debates, and speeches, are assessed.
- Assessments should be presented with information rather than numbers or letters. That will make assessments at the end of the year easy to understand. Grade level skills would be documented with information from the pre- and posttests.
- Having gathered this information, teachers along with the student and parent should develop a MAP (My Action Plan) that guides the student

toward their future. This MAP will be supported by a portfolio that will be developed throughout the years.

It is important to recognize that the previous high stakes standardized test is outdated and is too slow to get back to the teachers rendering it useless in the future. The small test will be for the sole purpose of finding a "jumping off spot" on their pathway to success.

THE MAP TO SUCCESS

To determine real achievement, each child has their own MAP as a guideline to their success. This MAP may take the form of a proficiency (or learning goal) checklist developed by educators with support from parents and the student. This checklist is personal as it gives direction to the curriculum and therefore to daily projects. As they complete this checklist, they know they are learning what is necessary for their future. Each check has an assessment attached to it which may be geared to a group or in some cases an individual.

Under this system, time frames within teaching blocks are not controlled by a bell or by a chapter test. Teachers, observing the successes of students, decide the time frame.

The student continuously moves forward making grade levels as well as letter grades, moot. If they "fail" a proficiency assessment, they do not get failed into oblivion. They learn from their failure, just as we do in life, and they challenge the proficiency when they are prepared. If it takes a little longer to learn, we wait for them. They might complete their education a week later, a month later, or whenever they achieve real proficiency.

If students move through the system faster, no longer are they held back just to look good getting straight "A's," those students have not been challenged. They might even move to a nearby university class in the subject area in which they excel. Under this plan, the genius in every child will come out when it is ready, and failure becomes a learning experience. The ability to fall down and get right back up is central to this philosophy.

Like the university system, students will have time to progress on their pathway to success. If learning is delayed and they are approaching 19, or 20 years of age, they will be able to continue their education at an alternative site such as a community college, a union hall, or other site designated to serve students of that age. This is an ideal spot for charter schools connected to a university.

While at the alternative site, they will finish their curriculum as well as take college courses if they choose. For example, if they are only lacking math skills, they can take that class at the alternative site, as well as university classes in other subjects giving them a start toward their degree or skill. If they drop out of school, they are welcomed to return to these alternative sites to follow their pathway to success. Their MAP follows them wherever they go, and they finish school at whatever age they are ready.

To prepare students for employment, skills training, or a university, high schools will provide information on specific skills needed for student success. This is not an SAT! This is real information in the form of a portfolio. Upon applying for a college or university, a student provides them with their MAP/portfolio, showing what skills they have achieved. Students are then accepted based on facts. Of course, other concerns would be addressed.

If potential university students are denied admittance, the college or university would say the student's weaknesses. At that point, the student could either choose a different college or university, or they could go to a community or alternative site to improve the skills necessary and reapply later. This can also work for employment. Students present their MAP/portfolio to the employer. The employer than decides if the student has sufficient skills for the job. If more skills are necessary, the student gains these skills and reapplies.

THE PORTFOLIO

Developing a portfolio of a student's best work is necessary to the development of their MAP and thus the essence of the new philosophy. This is their pathway to success. No longer does the standardized test drive the curriculum, now the collaboration between student, parent, and teacher will enhance the basic curriculum that is prepared at the school level with strong input from teachers. No more board members trying to force their agendas on unwitting students thus controlling their minds.

This process also holds universities accountable. If they turn down students, they must explain why.

The portfolios are a catalog of actual work, controlled by the student and parent and guided by the teacher. The portfolio is developed by challenging every student to collect samples of the work of which they are most proud. This begins in the students first year of school, likely at age five or six. The portfolio is then updated as students move on. Throughout the years, students begin to be mindful that they may be showing it to universities or potential employers. It is the time for the student to put their best face forward as the portfolio becomes the story of the student's educational life.

As the student matures, the contents are adjusted to meet the student's needs. This may be done after completion of their high school education. At that point they are encouraged to keep their best work, whether it is in their main portfolio, or not. As you look at the evolution of the portfolio you will see how it drives the learning process. Here are some thoughts:

- The portfolio process begins by collecting and dating all relevant work completed throughout the year as chosen by the parent and student and guided by the teacher. During the first year of the new process, students will do their best to update information from previous years. The process of adding new information will begin as soon as possible.
- This lends itself to thematic learning where students would collect their best information central to the theme. It may also be done at the end of a unit.
- Students are taught to compare their work with that of previous years. They will learn how to look for progress in their comparisons.
- Photos, videos, and other medias may be connected to their portfolio.

As students add and delete information, their portfolio becomes more focused and more specific to the needs of the student. As that evolves, it turns into a major part of the student's ongoing assessment.

ALL STUDENTS FITTING IN

The question then may arise, where do students with special education needs fit in? This group, often forgotten or pushed to the side, will fit perfectly into the new system of education. Remember, we now take children from "where they are," following their MAP and serving the needs of all.

What is a MAP? It is My Action Plan and is similar to an IEP, an Individual Education Plan, used to guide the special needs students on their pathway to success. Now everyone has that MAP/IEP: Now students with special education needs are no longer branded on their foreheads for all to see. No longer will top down, Common Core–style goals force teachers to compromise the IEPs to meet their demands.

NO MORE WALKING BILLBOARDS

Special education has evolved over the years but has never seemed to settle in as an integral part of the total education system. It has always been perceived as an asterisk to the general education provided. In the 1970s, special education was becoming an issue of interest for the first time. New laws were written to assure students with special education needs had a free and appropriate education. Although people were supportive of this effort, few understood its implications.

In past years, it would be commonplace for a visitor to be directed to the special education room. It was easy to find, you just take the staircase to the basement and look for the room with a sign designating it as the "Special Education Room," in clear letters. This level of advertising is not comforting to the students who inhabit that room. We know every child is different and some have more educational needs than others. However, they have an absolute right to confidentiality.

From the days of "normalization" as a key word to today's "inclusion," the result was the words all mean the same thing. Superficial actions of faux inclusion give the appearance that all students are doing well while they are in a regular classroom being taught in a way that isn't successful for the general education students, much less those with special education needs.

The fiasco of inclusion will be the first to be rearranged under this new system design. When all students have a plan in the form of the MAP, all student needs are foremost in the minds of educators. In the new system, inclusion will be turned upside down as all students will be received in a routine manner. They will proceed to teams with the expectation that students and educators alike will not only treat them in an appropriate manner but will be sensitive to their needs.

If any students have a specific area of need within this less restrictive classroom, a variety of techniques could be utilized. The normal classroom day would already include differentiated instruction of many types. For more extreme cases the students could be taught in small homogeneous groups. These groups would be based solely on student needs and that includes students who have no special education needs. They would not be created solely for those diagnosed with special education needs, but all students would blend in, and confidentiality would be maintained.

Those with special education needs would fit in perfectly. Of course, there are students whose needs include an even more restrictive setting. This would be honored as would all recommendations in the IEP / MAP. There are several key issues here that must be addressed. One is that students with special education needs would not be branded like a walking billboard. That includes no designated special education classroom or wings as well as not introducing the teachers as special education teachers.

Not only must we assure students are in their least restrictive environment, but they are serviced appropriately. The goal is not to simply have them fit in with a general education curriculum that isn't even appropriate for general education students. That means the system of education must change for all students. That community experiences, demonstrations of learning, projects, and a whole host of other learning strategies must be in place as they serve all students well. This must become a school where all children come to school as children, not branded as failures as soon as they enter the building.

Inclusion in a regular class would require that class be taught in the way all students learn best. The strategies of the past do not work for anyone.

SYSTEMIC CHANGE

Changing the system and philosophy of education will be exciting to some and scary to others. For most it will be both exciting and scary, as the way education has been perceived for the last 200 years will no longer exist. This change demands a new way of thinking. No longer may we celebrate artificial grades and grade point averages. No longer will we demean failure identified as student stupidity. The goal is to bring out the genius in every child. And failure is a giant step toward that goal.

Now, students will celebrate success at every level. Every former honor student will be acknowledged when they fail and overcome that failure as they reach for the stars. Those who were considered failures in the past will see hope in the future. And that hope will lead to a celebration when students reach a new level of achievement.

THE EINSTEIN CHALLENGE

Imagine those straight "A" students celebrating success at the university level while only 14 years old. That is much better than celebrating them coasting through for fake letter grades. Even if they worked hard for those grades, they know they could do even better. Call it the Einstein challenge as they tackle those university classes. It is much more important to reach higher learning levels than it is to receive a letter grade that has little or no meaning.

What value is a promotion if a student with straight "A's" can be promoted sitting beside a student with a D-average? Of course we can give it a new phony name. The 4.0 average now allows for a 4.5. Soon it will be a 5.0 just to show there is a difference between an "A" and a "D." How ridiculous! Why is promotion a singular solid motion. Children don't learn all their areas of study at the same rate. Let children be children!

A student at the Milwaukee Village Middle School was saddened when he did not get promoted to the high school. His parents came in to change his school. The problem, as explained to them, is that if he goes to another school, he must stay the entire year to be promoted. At MVS, if he achieves proficiency in October, he will move to the high school in October. The family was excited at the prospect.

Instead of sitting through a full year relearning many skills he has already achieved, he could finish the proficiency required with every educational minute having meaning. He came back to MVS, studied his heart out, and moved to high school in October. That shows the value of systemic change. That change could go a step further. He could have worked on that one proficiency at the middle school level and taken high school classes at the high school. They were both in the same building.

PUTTING A NEW FACE ON FAILURE

In today's artificial world, failure in school is about the most devastating experience a student can have. If you do not give the answers the textbook wants, you will fail. Regardless of thinking, the answer is the answer. Columbus discovered America, right? If you give the answer "correctly" according to earlier beliefs, you will succeed. However, if you think deeply and give a better answer, the testing machine will mark it wrong.

After all, when brainwashing is at epidemic levels it is difficult to seek the truth. When you learn a poem in school that begins "In 1492 Columbus sailed the ocean blue"? And then you celebrate Columbus Day, and there is Columbus, the state capital of Ohio, and on and on. Under the new system of education, failure will lead to knowledge. Next time say it might have been Leif Erickson, or was it Prince Madoc ab Owain Gwynedd in 1170 who landed in Mobile, Alabama? Or was it St. Brendon in the seventh century? If you want to confirm this, the survivors of Brendon's trip remain pickled in a Boston Saloon to this day.

I wonder if they are sweet pickles or dill?

A great example of the value of failure here is the lubricant WD-40. The 40 in that lubricant refers to the 39 failures leading to the 40th success. However, in school, those 39 failures would have put you into the streets on a cycle of poverty. Whether it is Milton Hershey, Dave Thomas, Albert Einstein, Giannis Antetokounmpo, or anyone who achieved real success, failure was the reason why.

A test was given at a university and one of the statements was "Which is worse, an abused child or an overprotected child?" The student, feeling confident that all the other questions on the test were correct, decided that there was more damage done to the overprotected child. It was evident that this would be the wrong answer but the student, being a smart aleck, wanted to challenge the thinking on this issue. The reasoning was that there were laws and a system in place to deal with child abuse. There was nothing in place to deal with overprotection. Of course, the answer given was wrong because there is nothing worse than child abuse.

The unspoken truth is that if a student has not failed, they have not been challenged. How else can we determine the progress of a student than to take them to the point where they fail. And then the learning process escalates. The student takes on that challenge through deep thinking, analyzing, debating and, developing the conclusion that they want. This may not be the conclusion the textbook wants, or the teacher wants. At that point they must justify their conclusion. That is where the real learning takes place. Just go down to a Boston pub and look in the pickle vat.

Learning is a constant flow of problem-solving experiences driven by the reality that failure is not only an option but an integral tool guiding students on their pathway to success.

What if a teacher assigned the class a project for the science fair? And what if the teacher said the students would be assessed based on the number of failures they had and resolved developing that project? Who would be the better student? The one who picked the easy project, or the one whose project is more challenging? Changing the face of failure leads to an abundance of teachable moments that would not exist previously.

Putting a new face on failure will take an abundance of creativity. All students will not fail at the same time in the same place. One suggestion is that a student fails a project, that child progresses along with other students in that group. That is how we do it now. There is a major difference. The student's failed area will not be checked off the checklist. The student will be provided support at another time during the day, before the start of school in the morning, after school in the evening, during a school break, or on a weekend to continue their education on that one project. The teachers will have the flexibility to control this based on student needs.

AGE LEVELS, NOT GRADE LEVELS

Under this plan, grade levels become age levels no longer based on academic achievement. It is no longer necessary to fail students back to a whole new age level as promotion is based on passing authentic assessments, not moving from grade to grade. The goal is to allow students to be comfortable within their age groups for optimal success.

This resolves many problems. First, since grade levels are not an indicator of promotion, the issue of being retained or passing without learning becomes moot. They simply stay with their group. Second, learning moves from grade level to the MAP. This will allow a laser-like focus on student progress. No more guessing what to teach. From these age-level groupings, teams are developed. It is obvious that the teams will not be homogeneous by design.

That is the way classes are now, no grade level is homogeneous. After the coronavirus crisis, that is no longer easy to ignore.

Assessments become presentations and can happen as a group or for individuals on various levels. Either way they check off a proficiency when they are successful and move on to the next. Each check is indicative of a demonstrated level of learning as presented in the student portfolio. It will be necessary to provide individualization within the teams, allowing differentiated instruction to take place in many forms.

TEAM FLEXIBILITY

The makeup of the team and its flexibility will differ with every level—elementary, middle, or secondary and will take that last ounce of creativity in your souls. Here we suggest a structure for middle-level students. Elementary level will be easier and secondary more difficult. Fundamental to a quality school system is the ability of the teachers to focus on the individual needs of a widely diverse population of students. Implementing differentiated instruction, essential to innovation, is hampered, if not destroyed by huge class sizes. How can an individualized system be accomplished with class sizes of 45 to 50 or more?

Right now, the alternative for many teachers is to throw out education for children to catch in a bushel basket or follow a standardized script. Others do their best to innovate under unspeakable conditions. The demands of earlier reforms required individualization. They require that no child shall be left behind, but they put a teacher into a classroom where they are forced to leave children behind with no individualization.

Here is one way many students get left behind. When a chapter is finished, a test is given. If a student fails, they still move on to the next chapter never gaining needed knowledge. With every chapter the student gets further behind. Between eighth and ninth grade the student realizes they are totally lost, and they drop out. Actually, Common Core, as bad as it was, started educators thinking about a proficiency system.

In the new system, the student moves on but receives service preparing for the assessment missed whenever it is available. Learning is no longer sacrificed for the convenience of keeping diverse students in one homogeneous group.

The teacher must become an advocate, speaking out not only about class size as a general statement but armed with a box full of ideas that can be implemented once the class size is brought down to a realistic level. Instead of standing silent, following a script, educators must take a stand in the classroom and beyond. It is unethical to be silent when the best interest of students is the issue. Teachers along with parents are the closest to the child, and if they cannot advocate, who can?

This is the difficult part. Regardless of planning time or class size, teachers may have to dive through this window of opportunity at once and muddle through. Now is the time to shake things up and some administrators may not be on board.

There are creative ways to improve class size at little extra cost. Along with that box full of ideas, creative strategies to reduce class size must be in your cache of wisdom. A wise use of educational assistants is one. At the middle school level imagine a team of two teachers, an educational assistant, and a special education teacher with a double class load of 60. That would be 30 per class. With four educators on that team, a group of students can be broken up into four groups of 15 for best results. It can also be divided in many ways based on the need of that day's lesson.

To cover the major subject areas ideally one teacher would have dual certification in math and science while the other in English and social studies. This allows coverage of those subjects in a 90-minute block time. Of course, on the elementary level this is less of a problem. You, as professional educators, would then decide which subjects would be taught and when. If your team decided they would spend the week on a science project another week on another subject just for a one-time project, then that is what you do. There is no need for administrative approval. You are in charge and no other accommodations are necessary.

When students are working in groups, or stations, teacher support will be decided by the team members to assure all areas are properly served. This must be flexible. For example, on one day a group of 15 students might go to a business as a community experience with the science teacher. Another group of seven or so might work an individual assignment on the computer supervised by an educational assistant.

A third group of eight or so could be pulled out to a small room to work on a specific proficiency taught by the special education teacher. And the fourth group might be scattered around the room working on their part of a project taught by the social tsudies teacher. These activities could exist without a lot of administrative juggling. There are other realities that might be built into the team.

On a particularly rough day one educator might be freed to deal with discipline problems. Sending students to "the office" weakens the teacher as students look elsewhere to work out their problems. Teachers can do anything an administrator can do except suspend and expel. Once the responsibility is with the team, negative behavior issues will slowly decrease. When the team has the control, the students recognize this. And when learning is hands-on and at the appropriate level, behavior issues are dramatically reduced.

Well-placed educational assistants are a great asset to the learning process. Requirements must be that they have taken education courses and ideally are continuing their education to become a teacher. That way a school can develop home-grown teachers familiar with their school philosophy. With the addition of educational assistants as well as sufficient teachers, the class load must be reduced to a level that is workable.

Planning time is essential to quality education. Some say teachers only spend four or five hours in the classroom. Consider that television network anchors only spend one hour in front of the camera. Does that mean the rest is free time? Sometime the networks should show what goes on behind the scenes of a newsroom. More planning than can be imagined. The same for teachers if they are allowed to do their job. Teachers are professionals. To give students a quality education, teachers must take back their profession!

To educate every child in the way they learn best is essential. That means a ton of planning and minutes become at the discretion of the team. Of course, in many states, Departments of Education require a certain number of minutes in certain subject areas. If they still use that antiquated system, then you simply put the tentative schedule on paper including what the minutes might be. However, if they want to count the actual minutes, let them try.

In this school, blanket permission slips would be signed by parents at the beginning of the year recognizing this is a community-based school and short trips will happen on a regular basis. Those experiences lasting longer such as three-day camping trips, trips including more hazardous activities like swimming, flying to a destination, and taking public transportation a longer distance would require permission. This is subject to your school policies.

In an urban setting, a well-planned community experience could fit into a 90-minute setting. Rural settings might take a little more creativity like putting the block at the end of the day thus allowing block time plus after school time as needed in order to transport students a further distance. If you, the reader, like this, use it. If not, throw it out and develop your own. But never, ever go back to the failed eighteenth century education of the past. Remember, there is time after school, time before school, time on weekends, time in summer, or other designated vacations. Just be creative!

EXPLORATORY WORKSHOPS

Essential to this systemic process is flexibility. This will take creativity, but it is workable. A fundamental goal of this system of education is to even the playing field. Here is how a little creativity can open the doors to every child's dream. As we even the playing field we allow every student to take part in high skill-level workshops based on their interests.

In the past, those with good grades in some subject areas would learn advanced skills. Grades being moot, it is time to allow students to tell educators what their interests are and how they want to achieve them. No longer may we push kids out of school before they blossom. Here is how we get every child the chance to follow their dreams. We introduce students to high-level skills via exploratory workshops. These hands-on activities are two-to-three-week workshops giving students an idea of what goes into a profession of their interest. These are simple overviews of the profession.

All students are welcomed regardless of their skills and abilities. It is important that we never again only seek students the school system deems worthy. We never know when genius will unfold, so we must allow it to happen. A good possibility is to put a local Community Learning Center in charge of this. Part of their philosophy is to bring in professional community members to work with the students.

The emphasis here is "hands-on" wherever possible. When Dr. Temple Grandin speaks, she talks about the classes that saved her future. Dr. Grandin is autistic and considered a genius. Although autism is seen by many as an extreme disability, the reality is that, according to Dr. Grandin, in Silicon Valley, most CEOs are autistic to a degree. All brains are different. In the movie about her and in real life, she gives credit to her science teacher who got her involved in hands-on activities, working with her strengths. Shouldn't this be the same for every student?

These workshops will be available to all students, whenever they decide they are ready, and will be held throughout the year for designated periods of time with the intent of introducing students to specific high-level skills. Remember, this is only a hands-on introduction to a skill. As students learn about the potential occupation and visit it on sight, they will get a clear understanding of the skills necessary to succeed.

The subject area for these workshops could be decided through a survey of students. Let the students dream! If the child is interested, they will be accepted, end of story! This might be the experience that ignites the flame in their soul. Individual schools develop their own specific time frames for the sessions. These workshops would be scattered throughout the student's high school years, utilizing the time frames of their entire high school career to implement this essential part of the program.

Here are the fundamentals about how this would work in a high school:

- Students will be exposed to a specific high-level skill in exploratory workshops when they decide they are ready.
- Students will not receive a letter grade or credit for taking these classes. There would be no pass or failure. The class is informational for the student.

- Workshops will focus on "hands-on" skills needed for the various professions.
- From information gathered, the students would then decide if they were interested in pursuing any of these higher-level skills.
- Those pursuing higher-level skills will then enroll in those full credit classes when they are ready.

Of course, the workshops include visits to the experts in the community. This is a short-term program designed to explore jobs that require higher-level skills. Students will get an idea as to the requirements of high skill jobs. They, then can make their decision based on their experiences in the workshop. Students who have been labeled as slower will now have a chance to let their real talents show rather than keep them hidden under an obsolete discriminatory educational design. This is a student-driven activity.

Let us examine the case of Roy, a student at PROSEFAM School in Barranquilla, Colombia. Roy struggled through school trying to keep up with his traditional studies. Neither the school nor Roy felt he was ready to go out into the world. He remained in school, splitting his learning between two campuses. While at home he continued studying using his joy of computer games to motivate him. During a recent discussion Roy stated that: "I work at home. Helping those who want their games improved and also fixing games that were not functioning well." He is learning a craft that may guide him into a career, with his passion leading the way.

This school in Colombia is a small school in a poor neighborhood that enrolls children for early childhood learning as well as others at every age who have not been successful or comfortable in the traditional school setting. They demonstrate many of the concepts presented in this book. In Roy's case, they kept him until he was ready to proceed on his pathway to success. At 20, it appears that the time has come. It is important to understand that he didn't just get tossed into the street based on a fake graduation with a D average.

GIVING SUBSTANCE TO GRADUATION

The four-year graduation rate has been calculated by using the number of students who graduate on time with a regular high school diploma. An initial concern is the issue of "on time." At what point does the importance of graduating in four years or less become the be-all and end-all of graduation. If someone was sick for a year and graduated a little later, are they less knowledgeable? If they develop at a slower rate, should they give up and not complete in four and a half years because they do not count anymore? If a school pulls a child out of the streets and gets them to graduate a little later, are they a bad school? Graduation is graduation!

As we take the education process away from winning and losing into learning, the MAP will be used to add some substance to graduation. The substance to graduation does not need to be standardized, however it does need to relate to the skills the child needs to move forward on their pathway to success. Although many students will graduate with similar goals on their MAP, some will have goals specific to their future dreams. Roy's goal came when he turned twenty.

It is important that graduation confirm the student has sufficient skills to move forward on their pathway to success. Skills brought forward are aligned with the child's dream for their future. These graduation requirements are developed by the school system in conjunction with the state and are made known to the community. Parents are fully involved in the process and especially university students or graduates who are working might have insight to the skills needed to thrive in their situation.

Graduation must assure a student is on their pathway to success. It must have meaning to the specific student.

Chapter 3

Eluding the Failed Policies of the Past

We are currently in an educational crisis beyond anything we have seen in recent history. We are reminded that skill levels are all over the board now that students have return from the coronavirus crisis. That discovery made us aware that skills were all over the board long before the virus struck. Of course, we remember all the students we retained until they disappeared, as well as the ones we moved forward totally unprepared for their future. As difficult as those decisions were, we accepted the reality that the current system of education does not allow for much else. The truth be told, it has never allowed for much else.

The coronavirus crisis taught us that we now must change what a school looks like. There are way too many children lagging behind after their return to school to simply tweak the failed system of education. We may no longer whitewash this as the problem is square in our face. It is not only time to recognize the difference in students. We must act. More sitting time will not resolve the problem. To provide quality learning for all children, we must be sure we design equity into every area of study. We must elude the policies of the past in search of brighter tomorrows.

EMPOWERING STUDENTS

As we move forward into a new education philosophy, it must be understood that students are not just a receptacle of learning but must become a full partner in the process. As students take ownership in their education, they are more likely to open their minds to ideas presented. In the process they will develop leadership skills previously limited by an outdated system of education. Now is the time for students to acquire the skills that will allow them to be independent and successful in their chosen communities. It is time for students to lead into the future, the learning that takes them to the wonderful experience in the world beyond the classroom.

As we place a stronger emphasis on demonstrations of learning, more relevant information will be gathered. After every assessment, students must be appraised of the results and use them with help from their parents, to MAP their future. This MAP of the future is where the goal setting begins. Only when students have input is their legitimacy in the goal selecting process. To begin the process, students will realize that goals are guidelines for learning, not deadlines for the old fashioned definition of failure.

Our job as educators is not to back them in the corner with deadlines to assure their decline. Once they reach their goals, they are pushed forward by the fact that new goals are immediately set. With this process, there is a high probability students will take one challenge after another getting addicted to success rather than addicted to failure. As progress is demonstrated, another addition is made to their students' portfolio. They oversee their portfolio which allows them to experience successes in real time, as they happen.

Student ownership allows them not only to feel pride in their accomplishments, but it allows them to take pride in the successes of their class and their school. That makes dropping out an emotionally difficult process. They simply feel better when they are in school and knowing success is just around the corner. When students feel a sense of ownership, there is less in-school violence, less destructive action, and less disregard for authority. Ownership gives a sense of responsibility.

OPPORTUNITIES FOR LEADERSHIP

With an active curriculum such as recommended here, there are many opportunities to have high expectations in a wide variety of activities. Consider all the leadership roles students can engage in utilizing creative projects such as those presented in this book. Once students believe they can be trusted to suggest and develop a creative project, all would be clamoring for those roles. Here are a few examples of opportunities available either in the classroom, school, or on a community experience:

- Conduct planning meetings.
- Lead a committee to suggest class learning projects.
- Make and receive phone calls from businesses.
- Send out e-mails and texts to members of their committee.
- Set up for an event.
- Coordinate the clean up after an event or a project in school.
- Make announcements.

- Prepare and send out flyers.

This list could go on forever, from the simplest roles to the most complex. This allows true leaders to rise and shine especially as more opportunities present themselves. As you read the forthcoming activities, think of all the empowerment jobs at which students would excel. We begin with the most fundamental of skills learned in school. Our efforts begin with creative ways to address reading.

Students are not limited to a single opportunity. Rotating jobs allows all to experience leadership roles.

ENHANCING LEARNING

Reading is personal and as such we must begin the teaching process utilizing the student's background knowledge. As they grasp the words most familiar to them, they will develop a base on which to expand. To support the reading specialist, reading clubs are designed to reinforce readings that are familiar to them as well as on a higher level that will give confidence to the reader as they move forward.

Children are not standardized therefore learning should not be standardized. Take children step by step, until the light bulb goes off, then reading becomes everyday business. The materials used must be high interest for them as well as at their reading level or slightly above. As they develop confidence, reading levels move up and up. As they develop the joy of reading, they will begin to read everything in sight. As we fill the curriculum with creativity, we elude the past by forcing it out. No space is left for those destructive ways.

READING CLUBS

"Reading Clubs" is a concept designed for every child to learn at their best rate. Although some disguise these activities with different names out of concern about student's "fear" of reading, we call them what they are, Reading Clubs. When done right, students are not the least bit afraid of reading. Like the concept of "stop everything and read," the entire school stops classes for forty-five minutes or so on a regular basis.

Every educator in the building becomes a reading teacher to assure small class sizes. No letter grades are given and there is no competition. Students are assigned to the levels of their assessment and adjusted by teachers who see differences within the groups. Here is one example of how it played out:

A student we will call Sonny, entered a middle school as a seventh grader. He was placed in reading clubs and given a one-on-one nonthreatening simple pretest to determine which club he would be in. He scored on the preprimer level which was confirmed by his classroom teacher; and we moved forward.

Teachers do not brow beat children, they do not tell them they are stupid through letter grades, and most of all, they do not have them compete in any way. Never, ever will reading clubs knock the joy of learning out of them. Students were in groups reading high-interest articles but with words they could read. There is no interest in giving them a seventh-grade text if they read at a third-grade level. There is no interest in shaming them into learning. With a one-on-one, pre- and postassessment, teachers can stay on top of progress, and it is not, in any way intimidating to the students.

There is a myth that students would be embarrassed and would act out if they were in low-skill groups. In our Milwaukee Village School, that did not happen. During the reading club you could hear a pin drop in the school. Why? Because they could actually read the articles given. Secondly, class sizes were determined by reading levels. The lowest-skilled students had small class sizes as low as three.

As we got to those on a higher level, the sizes increased often to around seven. Those beyond their level had even larger sizes, up to 30, and became involved in deep conversations, including visits with students from other schools. You will simply never get low-scoring children to read in a mob setting. Class size is essential. Finally, and most important, the culture of the school was the determining factor of the success of the program. There was no competition and no letter grades. The joy of reading was the driving force.

Now did Sonny miraculously jump up seven grade levels and read into the twilight? No, in fact for the first three months he would not even look at a book. Until one day he was walking in the hallway when spotted by an administrator. Before being admonished for being in the hall, he shouted, "When will we have reading clubs again?" The administrator stopped cold, shocked by this unexpected behavior. "Do you like reading club"? "Yes," he said and ran off. Suddenly being in the hall had less significance. Now for the nonbelievers, this is a true story.

Due to the individual attention and patience of his teacher, the light bulb went off. Hearing him in the hall constantly pestering his teacher as to when the next reading club would be, was music to the ears. The result was that he gained four grade levels during the remainder of that school year along with the following year. Remember, this is a young man who gained nothing in the previous six years.

This is an individual example of how reading clubs support children in developing reading skills and it did not cost a penny more! We must give children the power to learn, to use their brains to discover and analyze rather than memorize. They must learn to find their way in life, as leaders down their pathway of success rather than followers only to falter when they splash into the real world of work, community involvement, and daily living.

Greater gains will happen, not necessarily in the next year but maybe the following year and sometimes later. If we stay with students, they will succeed. Today the pattern is to push them out of school before they have a chance to blossom. Pressure them into their own "suicide by street" and watch the cycle of poverty play out as the system continues as its purpose of maintaining the subclass.

The reality is that through the reading clubs, individual expectations are high, and standards become guidelines for success rather than deadlines for failure. This of course would lead to individualization in schools which is necessary for success. The main difference between this new system and the current one is that this one never gives up on students. An individualized school with no false letter grades, no artificial grade levels, and a failure system that is part of the learning process will serve all students well.

When the reading club concept was put in place at the school, reading levels were not prominently displayed. Students merely went to Ms. Brown's room or Mr. Collins' room to read. Most important of all is that students became more concerned with their learning rather than their grade level. With the proper school atmosphere, as well as anonymity, the concept of learning exceeded the concept of winning and education became real. Here is how it was done:

- An atmosphere of respect was expected for every staff member.
- High expectations were held for all students on an individual basis.
- Student confidentiality was maintained. When students went to reading clubs, they simply focused on reading, not their levels.
- Reading materials, although on grade levels, did not indicate anywhere what level they were except for coded messages to teachers. Teachers did not discuss it in public.
- Essential to the above, there was no competition, letter grades, nor was there shaming. That was the main reason for success.

For success, all recommendations must be used jointly. Any one by itself will not be of value.

The implementation of the reading clubs was as follows:

- The reading groups met three times during the week for 45 minutes or so.
- The reading-group monitor was either a teacher, student teacher, principal, counselor, social worker, psychologist, educational assistant, retired

teacher, or other educator. Every educator in the building was utilized to assure small group sizes.
- The students read trade books, articles, newspapers, plays, or for pleasure, and learned about new topics.
- Each group had methods for documentation, discussion, and review.
- As student's progressed, these reading groups changed to meet the needs of the students.
- Teachers provided the reading materials for each group at the specific level needed.
- The first few minutes of each reading club session gave the students an introduction to the reading material and allowed them to discuss difficult new vocabulary words.
- Finally, the reading took place.
- As with all classes, time at the end of the session was utilized to "wrap up" the day's reading. What did I learn today?

Depending on the size of the group, a variety of methods were used to assure each student had sufficient reading time. With 10 minutes or so remaining in the session, the teacher or a student conducted a discussion of the reading. The last few of those minutes had the students documenting their participation. These times are approximate and can be adjusted at the discretion of the educator leading the reading club.

ADJUSTING THE MATH CURRICULUM

The reality is different brains see things differently. Human beings are not all extensions of the same person. No longer may educators demand that everyone think alike forcing those to do well on subjects in which they are less skilled before taking the subjects in which they excel. That is not rational. Begin by looking at the outdated mathematics structure. Yes, mathematics is factual in its event. We must, however, explore what elements of math are to be taught and to whom. It is time to take a good hard look at the math curriculum.

Which comes first, algebra or geometry? In the traditional, yet irrational step-by-step process of education, algebra has historically been a prerequisite to geometry. That seems logical because many believe geometry is more difficult or requires the skills learned in algebra to succeed. But is it rational? That process does not take into consideration how the brain works. Dr. Temple Grandin talks about the differences in brains.

Dr. Grandin says that she has the type of brain that sees things in pictures. She was horrible at algebra and thus was not allowed to take trigonometry or geometry in school. However, she discovered that she was superb at trigonometry and geometry and went on to become famous designing cattle shoots throughout the country using those skills. With the help of her science teacher, she was able to succeed in that class by using hands-on activities.

Dr. Grandin knows the differences in brains and acknowledges the need for all different types of brains in our world. That is why educators must reconsider the "one size fits all" approach to the mathematics curriculum. After all, there is no rationale that would indicate whether algebra or geometry is more important to any one student. The question becomes, what fits into the individual student's real-life needs and skills.

An example of fitting learning to students is found in the quadratic equation. Not everyone needs to identify the axis of symmetry of the parabola, nor do they know what that means. However, there are many uses for that formula. Students not only must be able to work that formula, but they must also fully understand its purpose. As they understand the real-life uses of a formula, they will become more invested in learning it.

Where does statistics fit into the picture? Consider that basic inferential statistics might be more useful to the average person than algebra or geometry. Although inferential statistics sounds difficult, it is no more of a challenge to students than any of the other areas of mathematics. In the name of critical thinking, the reader is encouraged to determine the statistics through their own research.

Often, especially in political circles, a distortion of statistics is used to frighten citizens into voting for their favorite candidate. Eleven families are brought to the forefront, saddened by the loss of a loved one at the hands of an undocumented individual. Sad as it is, those families are used by politicians to strike fear in the hearts of citizens so they would vote for them. Fear locks in our beliefs and the lack of knowledge of statistics adds to the confusion. It is time to focus on math that can be useful in daily life and inferential statistics leads the list.

Once fear takes hold, it is nearly impossible for one to talk their brain out of that thought. The solution, however, is critical thinking. What is the probability of evil acts taking place? The statistics will give students a better idea of whether they should really succumb to fear or simply ignore another political deception. A clue might be that 11 murderous undocumented individuals is horrible, but when compared to 11,000,000 undocumented individuals in this country, this comes to .0001%. That does not mean that there is no problem. It just means dig into it, study it, research it, and search for the truth.

One would wonder how many students would sign up for a class in probability and chance?

CIVICS: IDENTIFYING THE OBSTACLES

Civics has been long neglected in the curriculum on every level. All that is necessary is to turn on your radio or television or click to Facebook or Twitter to see a distorted view of how civics functions. In olden days, the promise by candidate Herbert Hoover in 1928 was to put a "chicken in every pot and a car in every garage." He was elected for the next four years. The 1929 Depression made it difficult to even get bread in every pot and a bicycle in every garage.

Students must realize that whenever something is promised by a candidate, there will be many obstacles in the way before it reaches fruition. Obviously, a depression was a major issue. However, there are other issues to be considered, namely Congress. The question must be asked, how are you going to accomplish this? Whose Congress are you going to get it through? We must teach children how government works or sometimes why it does not work. The legislative branch, the executive branch, and the judicial branch must all be in sync for any promise to be kept.

Civics must be taught thoroughly, not only by reading about it but by visiting a session of Congress to fully understand how complicated it is to get a bill through. The United States Supreme Court interprets the United States Constitution, not politicians, or any other group. Students must study the constitution and in doing so, must look at the Supreme Court decisions that are relevant. These court decisions must be examined to help students fully understand our government.

In addition to federal and state governments, how many students know how local governments run? An entire unit in school could be devoted to devising questions to ask your local politicians utilizing critical thinking. This lesson can begin with the youngest students and move on to those preparing to graduate and preparing to vote. On the upper elementary level, a mock Congress could vote on a bill presented by students. Of course, that bill would have to work its way through and yes, it could be vetoed by the teacher.

Students must learn to use critical thinking to prioritize the issues that are important to them and then determine whether those issues are legal and can make it through Congress. Then they will determine if the candidate has the skills to get that issue through Congress. If politicians are expected to agree with everything every human being in this country wants, there will soon be a rude awakening. They say one thing to one audience and another to a different group. Thus, the candidates try to convince everyone that they are on your side on every issue when that is impossible.

Students must be allowed to utilize deep, rational thinking to truly make wise decisions. They must learn to prioritize their issues recognizing no politician will ever be in 100% agreement with everyone. That process must begin in school. The role of education is not to take one side or another in a political debate. It is to create an environment conducive to rational, critical thinking with the hope that students will internalize that and carry it with them throughout life. And they must go out of their comfort zone for the sake of truth.

Many academics can be built into every project on the individual's level of achievement. This is to get the juices flowing. Students then must be encouraged to become involved in the politics of their choice outside the school. Embrace the politics they believe in and learn first-hand as they grow. There are so many real-life skills to include in the curriculum that do not appear on a standardized test. In school the discussion about politics must talk about processes.

Any sign of a partisan approach is not acceptable. Remember, the goal is to have children think deeply and come up with their own answers.

THE IMPORTANCE OF QUESTIONING

There are many issues that can be taught in the school system, however, they all will not fit into the textbooks. To control thinking, states have a Board of Education who sit around the table for hours trying to decide what to put into a textbook. It is difficult to subvert a school board's agenda to provide real, factual information. If educators are to stick to the facts, the first step is to discard any generalizations. Once an issue is branded by a generalization, the specifics of the issue are lost.

The second step is to throw out the textbook as it exists today. No longer may the textbook companies dictate the curriculum. If textbook companies wish to stay in business, they can create a line of questions for students to choose from along with a list of a wide variety of resources. This will allow them to introduce subjects to students but never to dictate subjects to them. Imagine a "textbook" introducing a wide variety of subjects and the questions to go along with them. No answers, just simple introductions. The content would be monitored for fairness by parent and teacher committees, and of course they would survey all parents for their opinion.

Schools are continuously challenged about what to teach. Should they teach Critical Race Theory for example? That is a branding that has been defined in numerous different ways. As long as the generalizations remain a part of the rhetoric, they will be difficult to get approved by many school boards. As educators, we can study various theories and build them into the process of history and simply seek the truth. Research of specific issues would lead to students drawing conclusions. Research could be individual or by speakers who would address classes as well as an entire assembly. The students choose the speakers.

The job of educators is to encourage children to think, not to regurgitate the lessons taught them. And to think, there must be questioning. And that is what is missing in education today. Make a variety of resources available for the students to research, analyze, synthesize, and then debate the issues. For years the primary role of educators was to tell students what to think (i.e., "teach to the test"). It is past time to let those students do the critical thinking.

As the teacher asks questions, that gives direction to the students without dictating an answer to them. What is more important, however, is to teach the students to ask questions. An Albert Einstein quote: "If I had an hour to solve a problem and my life depended on the solution, I would spend the first 55 minutes determining the proper question to ask, for once I know the proper question, I could solve the problem in less than five minutes."

Think about that in the context of asking questions. When we take schools out of the business of teaching the answers and into the business of teaching children to think, we will have begun an effective strategy to create a school full of geniuses. Curiosity is essential to learning. Curiosity leads to questioning which is the motivating factor in creativity, critical thinking, and innovation.

In the debate of whether to teach Critical Race Theory, one way of opening the door to critical thinking is through questioning. Teaching to those issues, simply give students a question. What affects race relations today? Then turn them loose to research, analyze, synthesize, debate, and defend their conclusions. Teach students to research a wide variety of issues, and then let them think. Once the discussion begins, there is no stopping the amount of information that is presented. And one of the resources students may or may not choose, is issues included in Critical Race Theory.

RISING ABOVE THE CONFIRMATION BIAS

The nature of those trying to impose a political agenda on you is to strike fear into your thought processes. This happens daily in advertising as well as in everyday discussions. Do not believe anything, question everything. Do the math, do the research, and only when you the student, are satisfied with the findings, believe the data. In education, teachers must turn students loose with guidance to determine their own conclusions and then discuss the results. Critical and rational thinking is the solution. After all, what is the fundamental purpose of education anyway? To win, or to learn how to thrive in one's chosen community?

The greatest challenge of education in this decade is to prepare children to rise above the "confirmation bias" and embrace critical thinking. In education, we do the opposite. Especially in this day of "teach to the test," students are encouraged to regurgitate what the teacher or textbook tells them thus diminishing the need for true critical thinking. This leads to yet another epidemic. The confirmation bias.

What is the confirmation bias and why is it important to the future of our world? According to Science Daily, "Confirmation bias is a phenomenon wherein decision makers have been shown to actively seek out and assign more weight to evidence that confirms their hypothesis and ignore or under weigh evidence that could disconfirm that hypothesis." Simply put, a person seeks their personal favorite answer, while often ignoring the facts.

What implications does this have on education? The frontal lobe of the brain believes everything it hears for a split second. Then it looks at past experiences and other arguments to determine the facts. When the person is surrounded by those who are also victims of the same confirmation bias, irrational thoughts will be vindicated. However, if children are taught to use critical thinking, they will then dig deeper to search for true solutions to a problem.

How many times have we listened to politicians make such ridiculous comments even the village idiot would not believe?

At first thought, we are convinced those believers are somewhere beyond stupid. Although some simply understand they are listening to lies and go along with them, many genuinely believe the lie or conspiracy theory du jour. The reality is those who believe those crazy things are not stupid. They are intelligent people. However, they are victims of yet another pandemic that is just as dangerous. They are victims of the confirmation bias.

Why does this "bias" have so much power? This bias is not only strengthened by the comfort it gives but by those who surround the believer. When a lie comes down, no matter how ridiculous, if it is supported by their favorite social media, by the select friends they talk to combined with their effort to ignore a variety of news sources, they will continue to believe nonsense.

The problem, however, goes much deeper. In school, children are taught to respond to a standardized test and give the answers the test wants. Although there is some value to this, of higher priority is to develop rational, critical thinking. As much as good teachers try to give a valued education, as schools shift more to the "teach to the test" mentality, they pull teachers away from those projects that encourage children to think, analyze, and come up with their own answers and then debate them with others.

Everything the standardized test can require can be accomplished in the classroom, over time, with the help of small pre- and posttests as well as classroom assessments.

A shift in the fundamental system and philosophy of education would not only have a strong effect on the students but could easily trickle up to adults. When they talk politics at home, the child could easily pass on what they are doing in school. Maybe it is time for the children to teach the adults to think. Children, when at home, show your family you can think beyond the confirmation bias. Show them what it looks like. Remember, everyone has a confirmation bias. I work hard to rise above mine. You must work hard to rise above yours. Distorted thinking must not go unchecked as the results could be devastating!

> Do not just teach your children to read . . . teach them to question what they read. Teach them to question everything.—George Carlin.

THE ROLE OF THE ARTS

The arts have been a mainstay in societies—throughout the world and throughout history. They are not only used for the aesthetic value but for a means of communication as well as a look into history. If you look at everything from rap and folk music to classical and pop, the artist tells a story about them and their community. The concerns are expressed just as if they were written or given in a speech.

John Lennon penned "Give Peace a Chance," which became an anthem for the peace movement in the seventies. "We Shall Overcome" was the rallying cry of the freedom movement of the sixties. "Oh Freedom" was a statement made by the Igbo tribe from Southern Nigeria as they refused to enter the new world as slaves, instead, they walked into the water to "take them home" to a better place. The message there was "before I'd be a slave I'll be buried in my grave and go home to my Lord and be free." That message evolved from the Igbo Landing in 1803 and resonated for more than two centuries to tell the story of their quest for freedom.

A strong message resounds in many forms of the arts. Comedians like George Carlin, Trevor Noah, and Stephen Colbert make statements through their comedy to get all politicians to sit up and listen. Paul Robison spread his message through the arts. He said, "As an artist I come to sing, but as a citizen, I will always speak for peace, and no one can silence me in this." This was not easy. After a rally for civil rights, the Peeksville riots took place in New York State in 1949. As Paul and fellow musicians, Woody Guthrie, Lee Hays, and Pete Seeger, and his wife Toshi with their infant children left, they were ambushed by white supremacists throwing rocks.

The group persevered and continued their work for civil rights. Pete Seeger was building a house and came back to use those rocks to build his chimney.

Martha Graham was quoted as saying "Dance is the hidden language of the soul of the body." A message is sent every time a dancer sets foot on a stage. The artwork "The Scream" by Edvard Munch may express how many of us feel today. The list goes on and on. To the day he died, Einstein insisted that the reason for his success was that he played the violin. According to G. J. Withrow, his lifetime friend, Einstein worked on his theories while improvising on the violin. It helped him think.

Plays were shut down in many countries when they were provocative in nature in the eyes of the dictators, yet they kept on persisting. "The Suicide" in 1928 was written by Nikolai Erdman. It talked about Russians taking back their lives from Communism. It took Stalin one performance to understand what it advocated, and he banned it. It continued playing under the name "Dying for It" and could not be silenced. Artists of all kinds possess political power.

What if students wrote their own plays with a strong message and performed them? Or how about writing and performing their own songs and artwork, and dance, and comedy, and on and on. What a skill to be developed. They research, read, write, and most of all, think! What a new concept for the education curriculum. How about bringing in artists from all areas to educate through the arts? The possibilities are endless, and the message is strong. The arts can say what the politicians cannot silence! Charles White graduated from Job Corp in Greenville, Kentucky. He was best at expressing himself through poetry.

Who is going to be the next Amanda Gordon or Charles White? Who will write the next powerful poem or compose the next anthem for the next revolution?

INTEGRATING HISTORY WITH THE ARTS

The history of the world can easily be found in the songs, the writings, the paintings, in dance, and the list goes on. From paintings on a cave wall to a play, to an opera, to the songs of Pete Seeger, Bob Dylan, and the New Freedom Singers, stories have been told. Now it is time for the students to have that experience. Here is a variety of options for students:

- A student will write or perform a song or a rap.
- A student will paint a mural.
- A student will participate in a debate, forensic activity, or a speech.

- A student will perform and/or choreograph a dance.
- A student will write and/or perform in a play.
- A student will design clothes and/or coordinate a fashion show.
- A student will write and perform a comedy skit.

Presenting in the form of an exhibition or a demonstration of learning, gives students the latitude to choose their own personal way to demonstrate what they have learned, and thus the probability of success will increase dramatically. Here is a sample lesson designed to incorporate music and theater into the history curriculum. Notice the amount of creative freedom students are given to follow their dreams. They choose the focus point for their presentation after doing their research.

Objective: Students will be able to describe a specific turning point in the history of slavery in the United States:

- Students will individually research and outline the history of slavery in the United States.
- Working in teams, students will decide a point in history for their focus.
- Students will research songs from that era:
  - "Follow the Drinking Gourd"
  - "Oh Freedom"
  - "Song of the Free"
  - "The Good Old Way"
  - "Michael Row the Boat"
- Students will work in small groups to develop a short skit incorporating the song.
- Students will present that skit.
- Students, as a chorus, will learn and perform the song of their choosing.
- A video of the skit with the song, will be played, and a discussion will follow.

This area of study is rich with musical thoughts that allow students to feel the history rather than just read about it. A much better understanding of history will be the result. This is only one example. Think of the many other ways of utilizing musicians, dancers, visual artists, comedians, actors, and others to enhance the education of all students. There is a wealth of talent in the community, use it to tell the stories of that community. Here is a story, in song, that creates awareness of the need to replace the broken system of education.

"GENIUS"
Song by C. Lee

For those who do not fit the mold, who never get the chance.
For those with their talents hidden, who never join the dance.
For those who are not the chosen ones, do not blossom all the same.
For those at whom the fingers point, who hang their head in shame.
We sing for you we pray for you, let the change begin.
Ignite the passion in your soul, that is how it must begin.
We sing for you we pray for you, let the change begin.
Ignite the passion in your soul, the genius from within.
For those through all their trials, who are slow to reach their mark.
For those with no fault of their own, are pushed out in the dark.
For those who see the hands that push, from ones they want to trust.
For those forced to walk away, their dreams left in the dust.
We sing for you we pray for you, let the change begin.
Ignite the passion in your soul, that is how it must begin.
We sing for you we pray for you, let the change begin.
Ignite the passion in your soul, the genius from within.
Take the labels off their heads, let them grow free.
Empowered to seek their future, their new reality.
Take the shackles off their legs, the children still oppressed.
Stop the race to emptiness, let them fulfill their quest.
We sing for you we pray for you, let the change begin.
Ignite the passion in your soul, that is how it must begin.
We sing for you we pray for you, let the change begin.
Ignite the passion in your soul, your genius from within
Ignite the passion in your soul, your genius from within,

Now it is your turn!

FACING ADVERSITY

Having good manners is of great importance to the well-being of each student. People with a good cadre of character skills tend to lead a more productive and satisfying personal and interpersonal life. As students find their way through life, they will come across a wide variety of obstacles. In doing so, they will need the skills to overcome every situation. This lesson will not tell them what to do in critical situations, however, it does allow them to think about a variety of responses they could use to resolve everyday problems. Here character development is taught using a structured format.

PROACTIVE CHARACTER DEVELOPMENT

The initial step is to ask students what problems they face in their community. From their information, a survey is developed to send to parents for their input. Information is included from the students; however, parents are encouraged to add their concerns to the list. From this information a character skill of the week is developed. Here are some thoughts giving teachers direction in implementing a character-building program:

Objective: Provide skill building to enable students to address issues and adversity and then cope with personal and character problems that, at times, result in disruptive behaviors in and out of the school building.

Each week, a new character skill is taught in all classes and generalized throughout the school settings and at home.

- Character-skills assessments are given to students and staff.
- Skills that are needed are documented and placed in a calendar.
- Steps to teach the skill are distributed and presented to the staff.
- Teacher presents the "Character Skill of the Week" using a specific model.
- The "Character Skill of the Week" is posted on school walls.
- The "Character Skill of the Week" sheet, with steps and the evaluation sheet is sent home every Friday.
- Students observed "using the skill of the week" could be rewarded using various methods. Rewards are not limited to a specific skill of the week. Although lessons in character skills are structured, many may be spontaneous.

The purpose of the rewards is to draw attention to the skill. Of course there shouldn't be rewards for students doing the right thing after the skills are internalized.

A character skills self-assessment taken by students could answer questions like these:

- Do I know of different ways to avoid fights?
- Is it easy for me to make the right choices?
- Do I get upset when I lose at a game?

Once the needed skills are defined, the calendar is created, and the character development lessons are organized. Remember these are just suggestions. Every student in every school has different needs. In the community there are various and sundry situations that might arise in today's world. What do you do when someone approaches you with a gun? What do you do when a police officer approaches you? What do you do when someone offers you drugs? It is not certain that all situations have solutions but this gets students thinking about the possibilities.

Expect the students to come up with their own solutions and debate them. Teachers won't be there when incidents happen and every situation is different. The students will be familiar with the situations in their community. As evidenced by recent history, guns are available everywhere. They are not exclusive to urban areas or any other community. When students are in their community, they must be aware of options. Sad to say, danger could lurk around any corner. As always, take the ideas you like and throw out the ones you do not. Make it your own.

MANNERS MATTER

In Milwaukee's Bell Middle School, a program was developed called M&M RAP; Manners Matter, Respect All People. A small group of students was formed to lead the effort. They started by selecting a "skill of the week" designed to reinforce good behaviors. The students then develop a rap around that skill and presented it to other members of the group. This rap could also be used in the morning announcements to develop awareness for all students.

The students in the group would then pass out M&M RAP cards to those students they observed exhibiting that skill. A drawing was then held, and a prize awarded to the card chosen. In addition, that team of students would use a video camera to catch students using the skill of the week. This was especially interesting when they decided to use the cameras on teachers. It is so important for all adults to be good role models.

With this small group of students in the lead, a wide range of speakers were invited to present related views to the student body. To fully develop good work habits these students were "turned loose" to choose the speakers, contact them, and invite them to speak. They would also formally introduce them to the student body. Every opportunity is made available for students to practice skills necessary for their future. The lead group was rotated to allow many students to have this experience.

PROTECTING CHILDREN

As educators seek solutions to the many threats facing students, we are reminded that there are subtle signs students display when they are experiencing social or emotional problems. Regardless of appearances, students are often suffering deeply inside. One way that has proven successful is the use of journaling as a means of communication. It is amazing what students will communicate if they can just write it down in private.

It matters not that they know the teachers will read their thoughts. In fact, the most success happens when students are given a choice as to whether teachers would read their material. The most effective way to do this is have two piles prepared for when students turn in their writings. They may choose to put their journal in the pile that the teacher will not read, or the pile the teacher will read. Rare, if ever will students request the teacher not read their journal.

As teachers review the journal, they would write comments but would never correct the student's writing and certainly would never give a letter grade. Students were free to write. Although a topic was given, students could write on anything they wanted. In addition to comments about the subject matter, quite often students would make comments about their feelings, things they would never say in public.

One student wrote, "I really like how Ms. Brown helped me today." A young girl wrote, "I hate Bobby, he touched me in my privates." Of course, that allowed us to follow up on that concern. The most difficult one was when Johnny wrote, "I hate my teacher, I'm going to kill her." In further discussion, he confirmed that his thoughts were real. Appropriate action was taken and there was a good chance a crisis was prevented.

The use of journaling on a regular basis will surprise you as students may write their inner most thoughts.

An article entitled "Talking Race, Controversy, and Trauma" by Leah Shafer (2/21/17) from Usable Knowledge, Connecting Research to Practice by the Harvard Graduate School of Education had former teacher and school administrator Aaliyah El-Amin, making suggestions on how teachers can help students process traumatic events.

- Acknowledge traumatic events or circumstances. Bring up news with students the day after it breaks, even if details or consequences are still uncertain.
- Process and name emotions together. Help students identify their emotions through discussion circles or individual writing prompts. Describe your own emotions, whether they be outrage, fear, numbness, or uncertainty.
- Ask students what they know and what they need. Some students may have a thorough grasp of what is going on, but little idea of how it could impact them.

Here are more suggestions to follow when a crisis occurs in or near school:

- Teach relevant information. Where possible, integrate current events into lesson plans to explain to students what has happened.
- Draw connections among the various forces facing communities of color. If you are unclear about details, be honest with your students, and work to investigate the details together.
- Connect students to resources. Show all students, including those who may be affected by new policies or rhetoric, that their school and teachers are there to help.
- Connect vulnerable students with local lawyers, social workers, and advocates who can provide them with the assistance they need.

No longer may we pretend problems do not exist when they are thrown into the faces of students. Students are more aware of the hurt than they show.

Chapter 4

Exploring the World beyond the Classroom

The well-spoken advice of Albert Einstein encourages timely action to begin the search for the "great opportunity" made available by the chaos of the coronavirus crisis. The response to this crisis demonstrated that education could exist outside the classroom. Although not successful for all students, computer-oriented learning could provide some needed individualization. It is dependent, however, on teachers developing individual plans based on the needs of students. Simply offering the same computerized assignment to everyone would not be of value.

As we explore the uses of the computer in this technological world, we let our imaginations go wild. If we can use Zoom or WhatsApp or Telegram or a collection of many other technological advances to talk to our friends all over the world, why don't we use the same technology to teach Spanish by talking to students in Colombia? If planned well, those students would learn English at the same time.

Now we move forward from learning languages with the proper accent, to world geography. Imagine a class in "The City of the Dead," Cairo, Egypt, taking a community experience by visiting the medieval Mamluc Mausoleums and sharing them with students, sitting in their rooms in the United States. So much is retained by those students for years to come unlike memorization which can be forgotten ten minutes after the test. And the cost is minimal and possibly nothing.

Here geography, history, and foreign language are all bundled into one. The possibilities are endless when we stop chasing those controlled by word games and math riddles to live and learn beyond the classroom. It is important to recognize that this computerized approach is only a small but important "piece of the puzzle." How can "out of school learning" become a positive addition to the learning experience for all students?

An educational crisis that was magnified by the coronavirus crisis coupled with ignoring the education of so many Black and Brown children in the past, demonstrates the need for vast improvements in the way children are educated. Of course, during this crisis students were confined to their homes. What if students were brought out of the confinement of the four walls of their homes and classrooms to gain a wide variety of experiences in their community?

IN SEARCH OF TEACHABLE MOMENTS

To make education real it is essential to escape from the four walls of the classroom to discover a world of teachable moments. These moments are everywhere we look, if only we open our eyes to the sights, ears to the sounds, and minds to the ever-expanding world around us. Putting an end to the limited view of the textbook, the search begins to collect a wealth of knowledge available from the front door of the school to the moon and back.

LEARNING IN THE COMMUNITY

Visits to businesses government organizations, attendance at music, drama, and other events, volunteer projects in the neighborhood, as well as a wide range of activities are all valuable assets when preparing students to thrive in their community. This adds immensely to the skill development of the student. To gain the full value of a community experience, students must be put in the lead. Beginning by organizing the project, not only do they learn from the information they receive at the various sites, but they also learn by preparing meaningful questions as they research the project, analyze the information, and discuss it with a team of fellow students.

Once information is gathered, students will find an appropriate site to visit. The goals of the project will relate directly to specific businesses. The search begins at the front door of the school. After all, some of the best resources are those most easily accessed. To discover what experiences the school neighborhood holds, again put students in the lead. Their first community project is to map the neighborhood. Not only are students to diagram the streets, but they also identify all businesses and organizations in the area, regardless of size. Some of the best experiences could easily be at a "mom and pop" store close by.

DEVELOPING A PROJECT

When students are put in the lead, learning for life outside the classroom expands their horizons. A significant part of a new project will have students creating a line of communication with the personnel at a prospective site. This leads to transparency and a smooth flowing activity. The project begins when the student contacts the personnel at the site. As calls get returned, they go directly to the student. If a business executive calls, the student responds. If the mayor calls, the student responds. Thus, the project begins. The duties of a student team will be focused on the subject to be discussed, questions to be asked, and other skills to be developed.

It is amazing how many activities will include a wide range of skills that exist in every student's MAP. And most include researching, analyzing, debating and, most important, applying knowledge to the world beyond the classroom. Think of the business skills they are gaining even before they set foot out of the school. A project is developed with a connection to each students MAP in mind. Here is a sampling: Students decide to do a fund raiser to help a homeless shelter. This includes many duties for a successful activity. As an assignment, students research and discuss the problems leading up to homelessness.

This leads to a great opportunity to discuss the effects of alcoholism and drug abuse, mental illness including PTSD, the lack of affordable housing, unemployment, poverty, racism, and the lack of needed services. Imagine how many lessons could be included in one simple project as students are free to make great discoveries. As students are in the lead, they choose the subjects in response to the questions they developed with guidance from the teachers. A visit to the shelter makes learning real.

There are no politicians on the Board of Education sitting around a huge table deciding for children what they should learn relating to this project.

Now the student management team will prepare a letter to the shelter and follow up with a visit to discuss details of the event. Once their team has basic information, they will present to all other students. During this meeting they will make clear the activity as well as clarify duties of those in all student departments. This will also include a visit to the shelter by all to assure a complete understanding of the total project.

Students working on math, and more specifically money, will be assigned to develop and maintain a budget. This would include seeking donations of bakery items as well as providing ingredients for the "student cooks" to bake sufficient products to sell. They also use their math skills to assure there is always sufficient items on stock and ready for sale. Once the budget is developed, the student budget specialists will request an appropriate loan.

The "student cooks" will then practice their skills with fractions and cooking-related measurements and make a budget request to purchase needed ingredients. As this is a fundraiser, they will want to purchase quality materials at the best price. This will take a good deal of research.

The students in the promotion department must work with those students designated to take the lead in developing a budget to request monies needed for advertising materials. Once their request is approved, the student advertising team will procure the needed materials maintaining a balance between quality and a reasonable price. In addition, they will determine the advertising strategy needed to assure their message reaches potential customers. Management will then determine a location and time for the sale. The "construction crew" will set up the site of the sale as well as placement of advertising.

This is all accomplished with students in the lead. This is only a sampling of how a project can serve the MAP of all students. The effort here is to break down the duties in line with the needs of the students as determined in their MAP. And reading, writing, math, and all academics are built into the project. Once you put a reality base on the fundamentals, the learning escalates.

In this chapter we look at some of the activities experienced throughout the years at our Milwaukee Village School in Milwaukee, Wisconsin. These experiences happened just as they are presented and will give you, the reader, ideas that may help in the future. This school was added as an innovative school to the Milwaukee Public Schools. Take what you like, throw out what you do not, it is your school, make these ideas your own.

TAKING READING ON THE ROAD

Maintaining the philosophy of taking students into the community as often as possible, we combined the concept of a cultural exchange program with our desire to help our highest-level reading club students develop high-level learning. Teacher Mary Gale Budzisz empowered her students to develop the program. A 75-mile trip from Milwaukee, Wisconsin, to Beloit, Wisconsin, did not diminish the enthusiasm of the students who were ready to take reading clubs on the road. Milwaukee is a city of approximately 600,000 citizens as Beloit is about half that size.

Students from both cities chose a short article to share with their new-found friends. Apprehension dissipated as soon as the students entered the building and were given a tour of the school. Despite cultural differences, the students immediately became children enjoying the others company as if they had known them for years. It was important for the students to choose the articles to be read as they were the ones with the curiosity. The first article discussed related to Japanese internment camps. Both groups read and discussed issues concerning how Japanese Americans were treated in the late 1930s and early 1940s. All participated in the discussion.

Remember, the subject matter is decided in the classroom under the watchful eye of the teacher. Not by politicians.

Later in the year, the return trip had the Beloit students travelling to Milwaukee to visit their friends and discuss articles that related to interpersonal relationships. Again, apprehension turned to hugs as the second leg of the project progressed. As students brainstormed ideas for a culminating activity, one student insisted that since Oprah always gave a dinner party to discuss books, why shouldn't we? Moving into action the students jointly decided to have their last dinner party/book review at a resort halfway between the two cities.

The consensus among the students was to read Grove's *The Crystal Garden*, a book about teenagers getting along under unusual circumstances. Through a small grant, written by the students, they were all given a copy of the book. In addition, teaming with a science class, they made actual crystal gardens they shared with each other. The joy of reading became the dominant issue.

This project was a success, but the reading clubs did not end there. Centering on the needs of the community, their next discussion focused on transferring the joy of reading into neighborhood homes. Students wrote a grant proposal in cooperation with a neighborhood bookstore to provide a reading of a variety of books and then give those books to those neighbors and students attending. This book of the month format had the books read by special guests and copies given to students and their families for their home libraries.

One of the first and best reading lessons is for the students to be read to. Seek out well-known people in the community to come to your school and read to your younger students.

> I think the modelling of the readers was fantastic. To have people from the community to come in and read, that was a side benefit in that it did model reading for you. . . . Now, it is easier for you to read in front of other people, to speak in front of other people . . . Do you remember (Journalist) Eugene Kane? I'll never forget that. He was reading Lion King and he enjoyed it so much.—Carla Alyson, partner, Readers Choice Bookstore to Chante and April, students at Milwaukee Village School, Milwaukee, WI.

Whenever a situation arose that allowed Book Clubs to connect with other subject matter classes within the school, a cross categorical activity was developed. On this project, art and science were built in. An artist in residence along with the art teacher had students study the reading, write about the characters, and draw and sketch their favorites. Throughout the year, not one textbook was opened, not one chapter test given.

No more may the textbook companies and politicians control the limited information that can fit into a textbook. Have students research the tough problems and then defend their answers. Let the students decide, through their research, what information will be shared with the class. Although teacher guidance was there when needed, seldom was it necessary as the students were thoughtful in their decisions.

STAY TUNED FOR A PUBLIC SERVICE ANNOUNCEMENT

Television programs infiltrate the lives of every student on a regular basis. Wouldn't it be valuable to understand the behind-the-scenes workings of this craft? Television stations are organized into five basic departments under the guidance of a company president and a general manager. These departments are news, programming, engineering, sales and advertising, and business administration. There are over 27,000 employees working in this industry.

Now we approached this industry with an eye out for the variety of student skills that can be developed. Television programs do not just happen, they take hours of planning.

> First, we were in the classroom, we had to figure out a public service announcement. We had to choose a topic, violence prevention or anything and we broke up into different groups, we worked on a topic, we worked on a script, we worked on anything to create a public service announcement. It was like a little movie I call it. We came down to MATA and they showed us how to use everything, from cameras, how to edit, everything about television production.—Chante Strehlke, former MVS student

From the curriculum, this project covered communication skills such as writing, speaking, listening, and reading. Under analytical thinking they researched, analyzed, synthesized, and debated the subject. Under technical skills was television production, computer skills. Under professional preparation was leadership skills and under community awareness was the awareness of MATA in the community and its connection to the community as a whole.

Notice that the curriculum headings are not traditional. They are broadened to be inclusive of skills needed to learn beyond the classroom and into the community at large. As students learn beyond the classroom, they become inspired toward a career. The bottom line came from Prince Starnes, former

MVS students who said: "I loved being at the television studio learning about cameras, but most of all I liked being on television." Isn't it time to put in the forefront of our curriculum, inspiring children?

URBAN FARMING

There must be a constant effort to connect education with the student's background knowledge to allow for a familiar "jumping off spot" for learning. To accomplish this, we often asked students what their grandparent's life was like? What skills did they need? That often brought up a discussion of farming. Many city dwellers have a family background that goes back to farming in rural areas.

Farming is everyday business for those in rural areas. Whether they farm, provide services to the farms, or simply live in the area of farming, there is value in understanding the cycle of the growing process. Urban farming as well as suburban farming has been popularized recently bringing us to visit "Growing Power," a farming project in the Midwest. CEO, farmer Will Allen opened his "door" to promote the education of students.

Small groups of Milwaukee Village School students attended weekly sessions with Will to fully understand the value of nutrition and a good diet. Will's greenhouse had the whole cycle of the growing process open and evident to the class. There was a little apprehension when the students were asked to dig their hands into a worm tank but without worms, there would be a serious problem growing food.

> We are really trying to get you guys connected to the food system and really respect where your food comes from and how hard it is. I know you guys have grown some stuff that was not successful and that's part of the whole process of learning that not everything is going to be successful in life. It is kind of a nurturing thing, recovering from failure. As a farmer, I farm over a hundred acres. Not everything works out, and that's the way life is.—Growing Power CEO Will Allen to former MVS student, Willie Monroe.

Students learned much from Will. But if they learned nothing more than how failure is so important to learning, they will be successful. The current system and philosophy of this new concept of schooling reinforces the role of failure as a positive experience. Failure leads to successful products grown by students at Will's farm and shared with community members to make learning real.

MAKING SCIENCE REAL

While seeking business partners to support the school, the focus should seldom be on money. Often schools seek donations from various business partners to support their favorite projects while ignoring the true value of an active business partner. Businesses are essential to the community learning process. After all, where are students going to go after they are out of school?

The goal of higher-level learning must be to "apply knowledge to the world beyond the classroom." There is no better way to accomplish this than for students to immerse themselves into the various opportunities available in the community. One such partner for this urban school system was the environmental firm of CH2MHill. The company representative was engineer Traci Rabindran. She began by presenting basic information about their company's wastewater treatment process, in the classroom.

It did not take too long before this show went on the road giving the students the education of the flushing toilet. This is one of many projects conducted by expanding the science class. It is easy to understand how this lesson will stick to the minds of the students. All those former students who were inspired by the questions on a standardized test please raise your hands. Here are Ms. Rabindran's comments:

> I presented the wastewater treatment process to the students using a few household ingredients. First, I showed the students some dirty water by mixing blue food coloring and dirt in a small fish tank. This illustrated dirty influent that enters a wastewater treatment plant or, as I said to the students "anything you flush down your toilet, bathtub or sink."
>
> I placed ping-pong balls in the tank that floated to the top. This represented the scum that would sit on the top of the water. Then, using an ordinary sieve from a kitchen, I removed the ping-pong balls to illustrate one of the first steps of waste-water treatment, that of removing scum from the top of a sediment tank.
>
> Alum was added next, a common household ingredient used in the pickling process. The alum drew the dirt particles together and floated to the bottom. This represented bacteria that are added to dirty water sitting in a sedimentation tank to digest the small solids floating in the water. The bacteria sticks together and floats to the bottom of a sedimentation tank, creating sludge.
>
> I then used a cup to remove a small sample of the dirty water. I poured the water into a funnel containing charcoal and cotton to filter the water. This represented the filtration process in a waste-water treatment plant. When the water passed through the homemade filter, it was no longer blue in color. Adding a small amount of household bleach to the filtered water represented the last step, chlorination. As a follow up to this demonstration I gave the students processing sheets to review what they learned.

This was only the beginning. The final step had students going to the local wastewater processing plant to reinforce what they have learned. As this plant served the city where the students lived, they could easily connect with the lesson. The students enjoyed the visit but were not sure they liked the smell. They were certain to remember the lesson every time they had to "relieve" themselves. But would they drink the water?

SCIENCE OF THE GREAT LAKES

Science teacher Catherine Spivey was always searching to provide knowledge to the world beyond the classroom. She and her class decided to take her students to nearby Lake Michigan. All of the Great Lakes are monitored especially for E. coli bacteria. Lake Michigan is used for drinking water around its shores including Manitowoc and Milwaukee in Wisconsin, Chicago in Illinois, Gary in Indiana, St. Joseph and Ludington in Michigan, and more. Imagine how much drinking water comes from the Great Lakes. Regular testing and effective water treatment has kept the water safe to drink. Here is her statement:

> The students and I chose to create a website called "Liquid Survival" which would encompass geography, water analysis and testing, global freshwater availability, and the resources from which we get freshwater. This was a high-level project for middle school, but the tasks were hands on, and the students were motivated by the topic.
> We involved schools in the four states that surround Lake Michigan in water testing and in environmental site analysis. We all went out on the same day at the same time and performed the same tests. The data was then submitted to us from all schools to include on our website. The students were deeply involved in collecting samples and data and doing tests, including the dissolved oxygen tests. We even had a school in Kenya corresponding with us who wanted to do the same type of project on their lake. Students loved the project and wanted it to grow.

This is a phenomenal project covering so many curriculum areas. This project is relative today and in the future. All schools around the Great Lakes and beyond should take on a project similar to this, not only for learning but for the future safety of the water. With a water crisis pending in so many parts of the country, for a school to explore both the quality of water in the Great Lakes as well as the quality of water treatment centers is essential. And Kenya's water also might be helped.

Why wouldn't this be a worldwide project? Since the day Kenya joined in the water project, their drinkable water has increased by 12% to 59% total.

Of course, the project may not be the reason of the increase, however, the increase demonstrates the intensity of the search for clean drinking water is increasing. 783,000,000 people around the world do not have access to safe drinking water. Universities use research to support communities, why shouldn't K–12 schools?

THE AFRICAN PURPOSE OF MARKET DAY

Incorporating a wide variety of academic studies into a community project was found to be easily accomplished. After all, real-life activities are where the lower-level activities started. They were just trimmed down to fit into a textbook. When items did not fit into the textbook, they were ignored and tossed out as if they never existed. Once you open the gateway for students to dig deeply and research, there is no telling what they will find. No subjects are whitewashed! Art teacher Darrell Terrell tells of his efforts to broaden the scope of education. Here is his story:

> The African purpose of a Market Day is to bring a oneness among people. That is also the purpose of our middle school students. It allows for the education of students in a holistic manner. Market Day is a culminating activity where students demonstrate learning through a display of works and performances. The centralized theme is entrepreneurship through community, as well as social and political responsibility. Through this activity, students develop an understanding of cooperative economic systems, the importance of leadership and community service.
>
> Students also develop an approach to the understanding of government. In language arts, students demonstrate reading comprehension by retelling African folklore, identifying the type of folklore and its elements, and exploring the cultural connections represented in the story. Students exhibit oral presentation skills using appropriate intonation and gesture, by varying volume, and making natural eye contact. This is one of the whole range of activities where students actually open a marketplace, sell items, have musical performances, and practice the art of storytelling.

These are only a few examples of how the school and community came together to make learning real.

DAILY COMMUNITY ACTIVITIES

Community experience projects are an example of a broad effort to inspire students to live education. There was more use of the community daily.

Teacher Monique Brown took her students on a walk around the block and charted houses, their shapes and colors. When they returned to class, the students used heavy paper to design their own model houses. Mary Gale Budzisz took her students to a hardware store to purchase tools and flowers to help beautify the neighborhood. Students were given a budget and had to stick to it.

As you can imagine, there are many ways to utilize the neighborhood for learning beyond the classroom. Just step outside and you can count the ways. The most damaging concept, throughout the history of education is the test and the teach to the test mentality. That alone throws a major roadblock in the way of whole child learning. The kind of limited learning that has been perpetrated upon children for centuries.

EXPLORING THE UNKNOWN

The friendly confines of the school and community are soon to be breached. No one said there were territorial limits on learning. As learning has now broken through the classroom walls into the community, the time has come to transcend the school hours by taking students overnight to seek other educational adventures. There is so much to be experienced when students must take responsibility for everyday living away from school and their parents. Whether it is in the woods, the ocean, or places beyond, there are teachable moments just waiting for students.

MIDNIGHT IN THE WOODS

Every class had the chance to go on a three-day environmental camping trip, and every minute of the camping trip was full of teachable moments. In addition to the wide variety of MAP skills achieved, this bonding experience went a long way to building a student-centered school. Planned as a yearly event, overnight camping trips allowed students to plan together, play together, and depend on each other in close quarters. A simple midnight walk in the woods brought out stories of history, mythology, zoology, and botany as well as a wide variety of learning skills.

During the day a specialist presented an environmental program while at night the planning was in the hands of the administrator as the midnight hike began. Immediately imaginations began to wander to speculate as to what abominable critter is peering from behind the trees in the deep woods. Of course, educators did little to comfort the students as the experiences were too exciting to tamper with. With this activity we place an emphasis on team-building as well as other learning curriculum areas. Here is the administrator's take on that experience:

> The students, nervous with anticipation, prepared to depart on a late-night walk in the woods. Silly playing turned to silence as the "snipe" was described and our efforts to catch the elusive critter planned. Slowly we crept into the woods following what they didn't know was a predetermined path designed to allow for the enjoyment of the sights and sounds of nature.
>
> The sound of rustling bushes had wide eyed children wondering, what is it? Who is it following? Leading the pack of adventure seekers, the administrator was quick to point out what appeared to be a nest of branches, a clear sign that the snipe was nearby. A hush came over the crew as another rustling had this leader, credibility in danger, diving headfirst into the nest struggling with what seemed to be the largest of all snipes.
>
> Unfortunately, the snipe escaped the administrator who was muddied from head to toe in his attempt to catch the elusive creature. The walk continued with the observing of a comet followed by the various constellations in the sky. The project culminated with the observing of the Big and Little Dipper and how important the North Star was in those many years ago and even now when someone is lost. The sighting of the North Star led to the singing of "Follow the Drinking Gourd" and the history of the underground railroad.

Safely back in camp, spooky stories had the toughest of students totally silent. As the lights were turned on to locate the students, all were found in one single bunk bed, frightening themselves, being the children they were allowed to be. The team building was evident at the end of the day when all joined in singing "This Little Light." The only student that wasn't singing was one who had recently been moved to this school. Her silliness was ignored thus highlighting the importance of the team-building process.

ON THE ROAD AGAIN

A group of students in an after-school club for those most in need of support, decided they wanted to go to the ocean and see the whales. So they went not just to see the whales but see history live in Boston. The bus ride to Boston began the learning session which would culminate in a great, in-person, history lesson. Imagine the possibilities. No sleeping here under the watchful eye of teacher and co-founder of the school, Mary Gale Budzisz.

Not a second of education was missed with Mary Gale as well as other teachers on the trip, standing in the aisle of the bus teaching. And the students didn't sleep during the lessons. Knowing Mary Gale, they didn't dare.

So, what were the duties of these middle school students during that trip? Here we go:

- Kept a journal, completed nightly. (writing)
- Kept track of the trip on the map. (reading, map skills)
- Studied the states in route. (social studies)
- Learned noted information about Boston. (social studies)
- Estimated travel times. (math)
- Paid for the gas with $100 bills, counted the change, and got receipts. (math)
- Chose places to eat based on quality and cost. (decision making, math)
- Figured out meal costs and determined tips. (math)
- Used proper etiquette in restaurants and other businesses. (social skills)
- Went on a boat to see the whales. (science)
- Got the poop scared out of them when a whale popped up and looked at them eye to eye. (priceless)
- Packed suitcases. (spatial skills, responsibility)
- Were responsible for their belongings (responsibility)
- Kept on a daily schedule, especially awakening in the morning. (responsibility)
- Fitted suitcases into bus. (spatial skills)
- Got along with others for a long period of time in close quarters. (character development)
- Reported on the trip to classmates when they returned. (speaking skills)
- Wrote about the trip when they returned. (writing skills)

Riding through the states that led to Boston was a geography lesson by itself. The students followed the trip on the map giving them a better idea of the size of the states as well as their terrain. In each state they had a chance to talk with some residents and ask questions. There are never ending learning experiences when students are on the road. Sometimes the greatest lessons are taken for granted as they are right before our eyes.

Finally arriving in Boston, a wide array of lessons were to begin. They even participated in a pickup game of soccer in Little Italy with some kids from the neighborhood. Following the trail Paul Revere rode gave them a better understanding of that place and time in history. Walking through Faneuil Hall, built in 1742, allowed their imaginations to go wild picturing the patriots meeting to listen to the great orators.

Just as a side note, the boys on this trip were those who have not shown success in academia in the past. They were also inclined to misbehave on occasion during the traditional classroom lessons. Other than a few expletives when the whale stopped by to say hi, this group used proper etiquette throughout the trip. Of course, proper etiquette was defined and clear to them. Those great students, who had seldom, if at all been on a trip outside their community, had a great time. Now, years after that excursion, ask them about it. They will remember every detail. And then ask them what they remember from a standardized test.

Of course, with every innovation comes the chaos of change. Problems with scheduling and other administrative necessities will arise but it is essential that those problems are faced head-on. It is easier to give-up on the project but that is no longer an option. In the past, for students to leave the building for longer than the normal 45-minute class time, classes must be covered by a teacher. Either substitute teachers must be called in or current teachers were assigned to the classes where needed.

However, after realizing most community activities could be accomplished in a 90-minute time frame, the solution was block time be provided on all levels. Here teachers work in teams to allow students to go into the community for real life experiences as well as provide creative groupings within the classroom to assure students are taught in the way they learn best. This allows for differentiated instruction on many levels.

More to the point, with block time, teachers are fully empowered to teach. If the team needed a class period to last 90 minutes, it will happen within their team block of time. If a shorter period is preferable, teachers would arrange that with their team of teachers. If they want to take their students into the community for the whole day, that could be arranged by the team as the team has their students for the entire time block.

Just clear with administration, pick up and go and this administrator's answer was always yes as long as teachers did their planning and every minute was used for specific education connected to the curriculum. Given that the community is considered a part of the classroom, parents, at the beginning of the year, sign permission slips allowing students to go into the community on a regular basis. No new permission slips were needed as the activities are routine, and parents are informed.

Teachers, working as a team could easily prepare themes by which to help drive their lessons. Thematic lessons help put all team teachers thinking in the same direction. This allows them to build on all team members thoughts and ideas. This is where planning time comes in. Team members must have daily time to get together and coordinate their plans. This has been rendered near impossible by the complex schedules of a traditional middle school as well as large class sizes and planning time filled with other menial duties.

Due to the coronavirus crisis, politicians will be forced to accept the high-level of professionalism needed to adequately prepare all students for their future. There will be no more shortcuts. Teachers, parents, and the community at large must remain vigilant. There will be many efforts to drag back innovation. Many will believe that the old fashioned "field trips" are nothing but play time with no redeemable value. Reinforce that these are not just field trips. These community experiences are an extension of the classroom!

It is essential that high expectations are certain for all students and every educational minute is accounted for. Assessment is continuous at the classroom level giving constant feedback to the team of teachers. Now it can be said that the essential purpose of assessment will never again be used as a scare tactic. Simply put, this innovation allows teachers to teach and all students to learn.

Learning in the community is not only a chance to explore the world beyond the classroom, but all traditional academic areas of study are incorporated into every lesson.

BRINGING THE COMMUNITY INTO THE CLASSROOM

The adventure into the community is only a part of our effort to take education away from the four walls of the classroom. Now we seek out those in the community and bring them as well as their ideas into the classroom. This project begins with a look deep into the history of the United States. So much of history is shared beyond racial and ethnic lines. In olden days, heat was not a high-powered furnace. Often it was logs or coals in a fireplace. Essential to heat was the quilt. It is not surprising to find that it was also used for storytelling, very important storytelling.

THE STORY OF THE QUILT

The connection with the community is important in so many ways. In and around Asheville, North Carolina, is a trail of barn quilts on display. This project started in Adams County, Ohio, in 2001 when Donna Sue Groves wanted to honor her mother but was not quite sure how to do it. So, she painted a quilt block on her tobacco barn. Quilts had a great significance throughout the years, and this was one way to display her favorite pattern.

This caught on and barn quilts popped up all over the South. What if barn quilts showed up painted on schoolhouse walls? If lacking wall space, maybe making an actual quilt would even be better. Now we take a look back in history to the early pioneers as well as days of slavery. A school project was to create a quilt using individual material squares made by each student using ideas based on their own community.

Although quilting started as a necessity to stay warm, it evolved into many uses. Known as the Freedom Quilt patterns, these quilts were displayed as signals to slaves that they should begin to pack for the journey (Wagon Wheel), dress up (Shoofly) and get ready to escape (Tumbling Blocks). In his book *Hidden in Plain View: A Secret Story of Quilts and the Underground Railroad*, Professor Dobard advances the thesis that secret codes were incorporated into quilts that were used by slaves to help them find their way to freedom along the Underground Railroad.

In seeking history try: "Underground Railroad and the Secret Codes of Antebellum, The Slave Quilts." The Journal of Blacks in Higher Education, No. 46 (Winter, 2004–2005), p. 44.

As time went by, quilts were used to tell family stories. Knowing the history, students start with a 9" by 9" piece of fabric. But this is not handed to them already cut. First, they must measure and cut the squares of fabric. The student then creates a story about something from their own neighborhood. The student then depicts the story in a drawing. The student transfers their drawing to the fabric square and sews it in place. They then prepare a written story with their classmates, about the quilt. Once complete, they donate the quilt to a nursing home to use as a lap blanket.

CONNECTING TO THE ELDERLY

It is phenomenal to realize the number and quality lessons from this quilt project. It is also easy to understand how it would not fit into a standardized test. The next project is to bring in seniors for an intergenerational nutrition program. Here the school partnered with the Black Health Coalition of Milwaukee, Wisconsin. Earlier the discussion was held regarding students learning the polling process. Here they used those skills again.

Students go door-to-door under the watchful eye of their teacher to survey seniors to determine the needs of the neighborhood. Again, students take the lead in writing a grant to fund their next project. Students then hand-write invitations and deliver them to the doors of identified seniors. The grant pays for the caterers and transportation for the seniors to come to school for the meal.

The students prepared and decorated the lunchroom. When the seniors arrive, the students would introduce them and show them where to sit for their meals. Imagine this group of seniors being waited on hand and foot by, what they used to believe, were rowdy middle school students. Lasting friendships were forged there. And the students wrote the budget (with help), wrote the invitations, planned the menu, analyzed the cost, prepared the budget, organized the guest list, prepared the room, served the lunch, and socialized—all learned in a reasonably short time. Every step was taught to perfection.

A follow up to this activity included another interview with the seniors to ask, "What can we do for you?" When the seniors answered, the group set up projects for the neighborhood.

DEVELOPING A COHESIVE CLASSROOM

Team building is an important part of the overall education of the students. Not only do students function in a school setting better after the team building experience, but they also learn skills that can carry into their future. This gives purpose to athletic events. Not only does team building occur on the courts or in the various sports field, it occurs at pep rallies where all students are seen as part of a team. For a moment, they are one. Beyond that, many activities can include team building as part of the lesson. There is no better way to begin the team-building process than to head for the isolation of the wilderness.

TEAM BUILDING ON HORSEBACK

Student team building could easily begin prior to the start of the school year. This leadership training not only bonded the participating students together, but they also developed leadership skills that could be passed on to the class. One such project was horseback riding 45 minutes away from school in the rolling hills of Southern Wisconsin's Kettle Moraine area. The first 20 students who signed up for our school during the first year of our existence were the riding candidates. The project at the Village School was headed by teacher Mary Gale Budzisz. Here are her words:

> With parental permission obtained the MVS leadership philosophy was set in motion a month before school was to start. Students ventured into the non-threatening learning challenges of a whole new world in rural Kettle Moraine. Donning our hiking boots, School Social worker Bill Brooks, Psychologist Tim Fosshage, and I dreamed that this frontier moment would culminate in our children leading the Village and changing their community. Only time would make our dreams for them come true.

Think of the opportunities for psychologists and social workers to connect with students. Not only were they not sitting in their office, they couldn't find their office.

Team building can happen both in the building and out, and team building can also happen between teachers and students. Students took ownership in the school by rotating jobs. Helping the cooks clean the cafeteria was one of those tasks passed among the students. For doing that, they got to have lunch with the principal at a nearby restaurant. A group of five students were able to connect with each other as well as the principal in a completely different setting. The conversation centered around daily events with no school talk allowed. No Big Macs here. They had a complete dinner of their choice. Steak, fish, or chicken were mostly chosen.

Within a school setting a novel event could happen on a daily basis. Sometimes you have to get out of the box so far that you can't find the box. This is one of those experiences unique to a school setting. In most, if not all schools a cafeteria serves food to the students. This allows for serving a large number of students in a short amount of time. Maybe it is time to allow more time for lunch. There is an obesity problem in the United States as well as in many other countries. One of the main contributors to this problem is children eating too fast.

How about giving students a longer lunch period so they can relax, digest their food, and avoid excessive weight gain (on the middle school level, relax may be too strong a word, but try). In fact, studies have shown that fast eaters may be up to twice as likely to be obese compared with those who eat slowly. Various articles indicated that it takes the body about 20 minutes to realize it is full, and thus the student might very well eat everything in sight for the first 20 minutes.

In addition, there are many other healthful reasons to eat slow like insulin resistance, type 2 diabetes, and metabolic syndrome which could lead to heart disease as well as diabetes. Is that not enough to increase the lunch time to 45 minutes? Of course, we know that students can become more active after lunch and that is another consideration. However, good health trumps all.

Here is a solution that leads to healthier eating habits as well as team building. Back in the day, at Boy Scout Camp Madron, to be specific, approximately eight Scouts sat at a table for lunch. They rotated seats as the seats determined the jobs at which they were assigned. The head of the table had the best job. He did nothing, but he had status. Two seats to his right was the Hopper. He had to jump up and get food anytime it was needed. On his left, two Scouts were designated to clean up.

This family-style lunch was an excellent team builder with Scouts helping Scouts, everyone passing the bowls of food and a constant social conversation being had by all. With help from the cooks, this can be replicated in the school. It would be important for all students to be involved as the cooks would not be friendly shifting from cafeteria style to family style on a daily basis. Once the complete shift was made and maintained, lunch time will become an excellent experience for the students.

Student team building should begin before the first day of school. Student leaders, taking charge of their own lives, can be a most powerful school resource. There are several steps to the team-building process. They are described as 1. Forming, 2. Storming, 3. Norming and 4. Performing. This process relates not only to schools but to businesses, social activities, as well as sports.

Here is the breakdown for the steps everyone goes through when bonding together as a team.

- First, the forming stage is when the team comes together for the first time.
- Second is the storming stage, when students display their differences.
- Third is the norming stage. Students settle into the way schools are supposed to be.
- Fourth is called performing. Here the sky is the limit, or maybe beyond. Students begin to perform at their maximum.

The "forming" stage not only happens at the beginning of the school year, but every time another person is added to class or the team. As it relates to school, a new student enters the group who have already bonded together. At first all seems well as the new student gets comfortable with their new group. This can relate to any group. An example is professional basketball. The Milwaukee Bucks added many new players to their roster for the 2020–2021 season. This not only included bench players, but starters. Their record through January 30th was 11 wins 9 losses. Not exactly a record of a champion.

In the "storming" stage, conflicts arise which may take the form of a simple disagreement on one extreme to actual arguments and fights on the other. This is particularly notable when a student is removed from another school for behavior problems. As students get passed from one school to another, they start the team-building process over again. And the disagreements and fights again take center stage often leading to the removal of a student, to another school where the process repeats itself. As for the Bucks, they would win five, lose five, and win five as they seemed to be finding themselves. To their credit, locker room concerns stayed in the locker room.

The third step is "norming" and is, hopefully, unremarkable. This begins the era of creativity. Classes run as normal, students are performing equal to their past skills and the routine becomes established. As for the Bucks, they had four-game winning streak, an eleven-game winning streak, and a three-game winning streak tied together. For students and the Bucks, only their imaginations would show the successes in the future.

The final step is "performing." This is where students are primed to go to "infinity and beyond"—Buzz Lightyear, voiced by Tim Allen. Following the lead of that famous space psychotherapist, Buzz, this is the time to challenge students to the extreme. They are capable of going further than they have gone in past school years. Don't let it go to waste. As for the Bucks, their final games showed a record of eleven and three and a playoff record of sixteen and seven and an NBA championship. Now that is performing. Now it can be easily understood why Charles Barkley picked the Bucks to win the championship, even when the Bucks were down.

The importance of team building at every level will be the difference between success and failure in the classroom and beyond.

Never Give Up on One Student

As difficult students are passed from school to school, the storming step of team building often leads to the last step as the student moves on and on. The problem is resolved when the student gives up and drops out of school. If only they could get passed the storming stage and move on to the norming stage, they would begin to settle in. They would be well on their way to the final stage which is performing. This might take the full year which makes it difficult. Unless the student continues the following year, the process might start over again. The process might also start over again after a summer off.

This explains how students can easily get into the failing routine, never again to see success. In the continuous effort to "push" the student out of school, that student will come into the new school in the middle of the year behind on the subject matter. Now we have a student who is not only primed for more behavior problems but is on a track for the old fashion type of failure due to being behind in their academics. The child simply doesn't have a chance of success unless the fast track to dropping out is stopped.

The first step in the process to save the student is to develop a behavior plan that includes an active curriculum. This is followed by plans B through Z as an effort to save the student from the shattered system of education. As the focus goes on team building, there are many activities that will escalate the process. The "ropes course" is one example. Here the participants wind their way through an entanglement of ropes requiring team work to succeed.

As they gained knowledge of their community, students were asked what experiences they wanted and where in the community they could find them. The responses included horseback riding, skiing, ice skating, roller blading, hiking, rock climbing, bowling, archery, camping, flying, hang gliding, to go to the ocean to see a whale, visit museums, fly to the moon, and many more. Amazingly, many of these could be easily tied to a curriculum. Those that wouldn't give the administrator cardiac arrest were considered.

Yes, they really were together in the community and the community stretched as far as it would go. (We are still working on the moon trip.)

Chapter 5

Quashing the Testing Obsession

Let it be said loud and clear. Assessment is only as good as the information gathered and its application to the education of the child. Throughout the years, assessment has been distorted to give politicians a false belief that a high-testing school is a good school while low-testing schools should be shut down and replaced. This false narrative has been used to promote charter schools, for-profit schools, and other "quick fix" alternatives.

With that in mind let us look at the purpose for today's test disguised as assessment. That primary purpose ignores the overall needs of children to focus on a simplistic score. That score is convenient to politicians as the conversation goes immediately to the school. Which school has the best test scores. Of course, that must be the best school and thus makes the best headlines. However, that is not accurate on several levels.

SEEKING TRUE STUDENT ASSESSMENT

To understand the need for systemic change we must realize that assessment drives the school, as well as the student's curriculum. Currently the test is primarily designed for convenience and thus fails to be the powerful leader that guides the curriculum of a school in a good direction. Instead, it distorts the true needs of the student. It is time to address education and the problems of inequality in today's system and philosophy.

STOP THE RACE TO NOWHERE!

We have discovered, during the coronavirus crisis, that all students are not starting the race from the same place. As the students returned, their test scores were all over the board, mostly as determined by the artificial test. That test is a perfect fit for those who consider education a race. It has clear test scores, and those scores can be ranked and sorted and ultimately followed to assure every child is in lock step or failed into oblivion. That makes the politicians happy as they can fit everyone into their perceived mold.

But where are their skills when we assess the whole child? What are their educational needs? That is yet to be determined as the test has a narrow scope with limited and even false outcomes. What happens when education is taken out of the race to nowhere? Once we realize education isn't a race, one student against a test score, we will then begin to understand the fundamental purpose of education. To start each child, not in a race, but to their individual pathway to success.

It will be obvious to a rational mind that no grade level is an indicator of academic achievement. Students simply don't march forward in lock step, learning at the same rate or in the same way. Yet every school has the task to determine what grade students should be in. As grade levels are artificial by their nature, and test scores are not quality assessments, no one really knows where to place students. Under the current "one-size-fits-all" system, some will be retained, some will move ahead without learning, and few will get a quality education that fits their whole child needs. There is no grade level solution under the current system!

Let us now focus on the value of the standardized test for students. Does the test information apply directly to the education of the student? Let us begin with time frames. Often the high stakes test takes as much as four months to get back to the teacher. By then, teachers have long completed their planning rendering the fundamental purpose of the test as an assessment, moot.

Remember, the test is merely a snapshot in time leading to a "jumping off spot" for the student's lesson. Under this new philosophy, planning must begin immediately. Teachers may not delay planning for any extended period and certainly not for four months while we wait for the test scores. Nor should they make plans based solely on test scores. Well-planned, timely lessons are essential to reaching all students in the way they learn best. The results must be immediate and ongoing to assure and focus on the students' needs for their future. And the results, as given by the test, will be inadequate to change the focus to the whole child.

Dr. Nikki Woodson, school superintendent in an Indiana public school, wasn't about to wait four months for a high-stake standardized test to return to be used by her teachers for planning. She went to her School Board and explained the importance of receiving information in a timely manner. The Board understood and gave permission for all city teachers to do their small tests in order to prepare their student plans at the beginning of the school year. Here the Superintendent was found a way to follow the "rules" so as to diminish its role. Was that enough to change the focus to the whole child? Consider the flaws of the test.

As long as the test shows up in any form, the nature of educators will be to use it as more than a "jumping off point." That would be an administrative challenge.

Consider the mindset of students taking the high-stakes standardized test. Are they seeking out the best answers possible, or do they simply look for the answers that are expected? Often high-quality readers have been sent to remedial reading or other low-skill reading classes when they did not answer the way the test givers preferred. Students do not approach tests in the same way. The standardized test is one clear example of what's wrong with the system as a whole. Kids must no longer be forced into a single standard for politicians to use in their rhetoric.

The test itself is flawed in many more ways. To "succeed" on a standardized test not only do students have to determine what answers are desired, they must all have the same source of background knowledge. When a student doesn't grasp a question, it might be the lack of familiarity with the subject matter. Must that child then fit a mold as required by the companies drafting the test? Must everyone be forced to fit that same mold? One test for the entire country is ludicrous.

It is past time to scrutinize the issues that are essential to critical thinking. Just about every sign of creative thinking has been snuffed out not solely by the infamous high-stakes test but the teach-to-the-test curriculum that is attached to it. Children may no longer be held hostage to the narrow scope of the standardized test when it is necessary to understand the needs of the whole child. No longer will educators chase their tales, following like lemmings into the sea to be drowned in a tsunami of word games and math riddles. Major issues of critical thinking are missing in the big test.

- Is it possible for the child to fully research a problem with limited time as well as limited resources available during the test? The ability to gather a wide range of information is necessary for critical thinking.
- An important part of critical thinking is to ask in-depth questions. Can students even talk during the test? They must just search for the answer that is desired.
- Is it not important for the student to listen to arguments on all sides of the issue and make self-corrections? Once they bubble in the sheet, it is done!
- The ability of the students to work as part of a team to demonstrate a conclusion is not allowed during the test.
- Will they work with a team of evaluators to form a consensus? Not during the test.

Think how assessment can utilize these issues and many more to fully understand the future needs of the student.

HOW STRESS EFFECTS LEARNING

Consider the ability of students to focus on a test as it is essential to a good score. Anyone who has ever done a crossword puzzle will understand that on some days the words "pop out" at you while other days the true meaning of a simple word is elusive. The same can be said for children. If they happen to have a bad day on testing day, their future is in question. And if that testing day is highly stressful for a majority of students in a single school, and they are piling that on top of a stressful environment, the school will become a low-scoring school.

Remember Dr. Kara Fitzgerald's discussion about stress and its effect on the human mind and body. "That a stressful environment really coordinates three kinds of responses in the body: an immune response, a metabolic response, and a behavioral response." With all that going on, the test answers might not "pop out" at the student at all.

Earlier we discussed the effect of childhood stress on learning. How could there be any more stress placed on children than the approach used to prepare them for the high-stakes, standardized test. The pressure begins with the "teach to the test" debacle. What more pressure could be placed on the shoulders of unsuspecting students than to design the curriculum, taught throughout the year, with the primary purpose of getting a good test score?

Every day a "teach-to-the-test" scripted lesson is taught, the rubber band that drives many students "memorizing propeller" stretches further and further until on testing day it either snaps or spins out of control. Drawing up those memorized answers or formulas becomes more difficult for some students and impossible for others. This school stress on top of stresses from the neighborhood have a debilitating effect on students.

Now we approach testing day. A voice blares out through a public announcement system, "Tomorrow is test day. Make sure you get a lot of rest, eat a good breakfast, and come to school ready to take the test that may influence the rest of your life. Now, go home and relax!" Try to sleep with that announcement buzzing around in your head. If any student has self-doubts, they will immediately be brought to the surface.

Now comes testing day and the school atmosphere is tense to say the least. This one and only day will determine your future students are told. Teachers see students 150 to 200 days a year, yet a single test on a single day, in a single subject is prioritized in the minds of teachers and students. Childhood stress is at the maximum. This test is about winning, a true assessment is about learning. When it is about learning, the focus is on the accurate gathering of information rather than jumping through hoops.

When a test is about winning, there will be cheating, as evidenced by recent history. Assessment must be about learning, then there will be no reason to cheat.

The book *Choke*, Simon and Schuster, 2010, was written by Dr. Sian Beilock. In her book she asks the question "Why do we sometimes fail to perform at our best when it counts the most." She talks about her friend Abby who did better on the LSAT than she did on her sample tests. And that many who do well on the sample tests, do poorly on the actual test. This is telling, as she states: "in that one day, that one four-hour test Abby was admitted to the best law school in the country, had a leading firm recruiting her by the end of her first year and landed a high paying job when she graduated."

According to Dr. Beilock, this was partially due to a single test on a single day, the LSAT. Do we see any pressure there? Her friend Abby was able to handle the stress of the main test but was possibly over thinking on the sample tests. The important take away from this is how the brain functions differently in every human being. Abby's brain was structured so that she can rise to pressure situations.

In children, however, there are many other issues in play. High stress, lack of sleep, malnutrition, and other demands of the child do their share of damage. As the brain must adjust to this wide variety of issues, it could also be hampered by lead paint, trauma due to an accident, problems at or before birth, and a host of many other concerns. Now, as educators, do we focus more on teaching students how to handle a stressful situation?

As a solution, do we get rid of the high-stakes test and other high-stress situations? Do we do both stress elimination and teach how to handle it? Or do we continue to pretend the problem doesn't exist using excuses such as "poverty is not destiny" or "it is the teachers fault?" All these fake responses have a primary purpose of, according to Thomas Jefferson, "raking a few geniuses from the rubbish." In other words, pushing more and more children out of school to struggle with daily life in poverty or jump into the school-to-prison pipeline.

We must take a hard look at the consequences of children doing poorly in high-stress situations. Special attention is required when a high-stress activity is piled upon a whole array of stressors the child faces before they get to school. The loss of a quality future for a child is unacceptable. So, do we show kids how to handle stress? That might be a good idea. Do we eliminate high-stress situations? That depends on the potential damage.

High stress in a basketball game, a debate, orchestra competition, or other similar events would be a good way to teach students how to deal with stressful situations. In these activities, the most the child has to lose is a game or a meet. But when the child has their future to lose, the relative importance of the stressful situation must be considered. On a standardized test, there are 150 to 200 more ways to gather information in less stressful situations. Those would be the days teachers see the students.

For those who believe that the high-stress test is preparing them for the SAT, failure could very well beget more failure.

Dr. Beilock goes on stating: "choking occurs in a response to a highly stressful situation." This is a familiar theme consistent with the works of Dr. Kara Fitzgerald. High stress is built into the current system and philosophy of education as much depends on the high-stakes standardized test as well as a system of testing rather than a system of assessment. Add that to the stress of a child's home environment and the results are not good.

Many readers may identify with what Dr. Beilock calls "Paralysis by Analysis." Simply put this is when we over think a process that is usually automatic. Another issue is when the test taker is not paying enough attention to the issue at hand. No matter the reason, a high-stakes test for K–12 students is a horrible way to gather information. Dr. Beilock goes into detail in her book. Those who read that book will never again think the same way about education.

The deeper we get into understanding learning, the more we understand that there are many theories spewed out that are simply political rhetoric. Most notable is "poverty is not destiny." The intelligent move is to consult the experts who have studied the effects of stress and other roadblocks to learning, rather than to pretend to have total knowledge of scientific issues. Assessment must approach children in a reasonable manner focusing on a new reality that one test will no longer be allowed to destroy a student. It's about learning.

ASSESSMENT BY EXHIBITION

The days of the chapter test are over. A demonstration of learning is often the best way to assess what students really know. The exhibition is one way of assessing students by demonstrating their skills in the way they do it best. It may take the form of a speech, a play, a song, a debate, a project, or any other means by which the student can truly show what they can do, in the way they do it best.

We begin by assuring teachers have a full understanding of the concept of the exhibition. Exhibitions are an activity used for students to demonstrate learned proficiencies; therefore, it is essential that they connect to the students MAP. While exhibitions can occur based on the needs of students, it is also valuable to have them as a culminating activity to a thematic unit. Although students are in the lead, teachers will act as facilitators and then step aside to let the students shine. It may take a few exhibitions for the students to get the real idea, but soon they will know how to take the reins and will amaze the audience with what they have learned.

Under the careful eye of the teachers, students will prepare every aspect of the exhibition with a focus on the MAP goals they choose.

Empowering students to understand how they are progressing on their proficiency checklist requires a self-assessment. This will reinforce their view of what they have learned. When they return home after school and are asked, "What did you learn in school today?", they will be able to answer in a reasonable manner. Here are some sample questions and answers to give you ideas for self-assessments:

- State the specific role that I played in this Exhibition:
  - "I helped make the set, the costumes, and was the moderator for this Exhibition."
  - "What proficiency did I exhibit? Analytical Thinking."
  - Math: "I designed and measured the cloth for my costume."
- Communication Skills:
  - Speaking: "I prepared and delivered a commentary within the setting of a play."
  - Reading: "I researched the history related to my role in the play."
  - Writing: "I wrote out my script."
  - Listening: "I listened to other cast members to better understand how my character fit into the overall play."
  - The Arts: "I used dance to tell a story of a historical event."

Students should assess themselves on how well they did on this activity. This could be enhanced by a small group discussion with peers to get their perception of issues like eye contact, a loud and clear voice, command of the language, and a display of confidence as well as other concerns. It is especially helpful to have a video of the presentation to assist in the self-assessment.

This self-assessment is a great review to use in the last few minutes of every class lesson. It assures information is clear to students. If doubts exist, questions are asked until the day's lesson is clear.

Many other issues could easily be a part of the self-assessment. Most important is for the student to look inward and recognize what they did well and where they "failed." As with WD-40, that failure then becomes part of the learning process. As others assess students, it is critical that the assessment is focused on the student MAP needs. Although many of the students will have similar assessment needs, some needs will be specific to the individual. It is essential for students to identify those needs as goals and for the teacher to indicate student progress toward them. Teacher assessment of students will focus on the specifics of their MAP with general considerations:

- Did the student address the proficiency?
- Did they present a clear understanding of the subject matter?
  - Document the specifics. Did the student present sufficient information to achieve proficiency?
  - If they did not achieve proficiency, specifically what skills do they need to demonstrate to achieve success.
- When will they have the next opportunity to demonstrate the proficiency?

A teacher review of a video is valuable to reinforce a critical evaluation.

ADDRESSING CRITICAL THINKING

How do we assess critical thinking? With critical thinking the importance is not who wins or loses, it is what is learned and what will be learned from the failures that are now positive learning experiences. Assessing a project includes a wide range of methods used to demonstrate skills and abilities. Assess this project, not with letter grades, but with observations of every aspect of the child's performance with a special emphasis on their MAP objectives. Projects are a creative way to assess children. Assessing critical thinking, we now take note of what Dr. Angela Dye referred to as "A" level learning to develop an assessment outline.

- Analyzing
  - Define the central issues of the problem.
  - Fully understand the complexity of the problem.
  - Resources needed to resolve the issue at hand.
  - Research the problem.
- Synthesizing
  - Ask pertinent questions relative to the problem.
  - Identify arguments on all sides of the issue.
  - Make self-corrections.
  - Correctly interpret data.
- Applying
  - Identify the problem.
  - Make the case for your designated argument.
  - Draw and support valid conclusions.
  - Examples and facts are given to support reasons, with references.
  - Work as a team to demonstrate or present YOUR conclusions.

- Evaluating
  - Evaluating the reliability of evidence.
  - Evaluate the validity of your conclusions.
  - Work with a team of evaluators to come to a consensus.

Every student must be challenged to reach their ultimate level of achievement. When the politicians try to draw you back to a testing mentality, remind them that we can assess orchestra competitions, science fairs, forensics meets, singers on "The Voice," speeches, and many more activities in a meaningful way without using the high stakes test. The test is the worst way to determine a student's skills.

If children grew up to be analytical in their thinking, the world would be a much better place, and lies and distortions would no longer be commonplace.

Throughout life we have good days where we have a strong focus and bad days where our focus has diminished. This is one reason a singular standardized test lacks value. Student assessment comes in many forms. Looking at the "Every Child Succeeds Act" we see some supportive developments as follows:

A new demonstration authority under which an SEA or consortium of SEAs that meets certain application requirements may establish, operate, and evaluate an innovative assessment system, including for use in the statewide accountability system, with the goal of using the innovative assessment system after the demonstration authority ends to meet the academic assessment and statewide.

a. Innovative assessment system defined:

The term "innovative assessment system" means a system of assessments that may include:
1. Competency-based assessments, instructionally embedded assessments, interim assessments, cumulative year end assessments, or performance-based assessments that combine into an annual summative determination for a student which may be administered through computer adapted assessments and
2. Assessments that validate when students are ready to demonstrate mastery or proficiency and allow for differentiated student support based on individual learning needs.

This portion of the bill has the potential of being a game changer. Performance-based assessments may be unique and fit our new philosophy. Instructionally embedded assessments appear to allow teachers flexibility and assessments based on differentiated student support based on individual learning needs. And if their educational leads to their MAP, which shows mastery of their proficiencies, then the curriculum will change drastically for each student. Included are performance-based assessments. Again, the curriculum must now prepare students to demonstrate learning, not simply take the test. Let your imagination go wild. Your permission is there in law!

Of course, these laws are amended on a regular basis and may be gone in a New York second.

SCHOOL ACCOUNTABILITY

There are many facets to the educational crisis and systemic change is high on that list. The past has politicians taking the easiest route to school accountability. However, the easiest route lacks validity. The standardized test, in no way can be effectively used to determine the quality of a school. As previously explained, the test is flawed in many ways. As it is not a quality method of "assessing" children, it simply may not be an effective way of "assessing" schools.

In addition to the lack of validity, students may enter the school at different times. As tests are based mainly on memorization of information, will the same information be given to students who begin the year in September as compared to those who begin in May? This is simply another reason to eliminate the test as an indicator of school or student achievement. It is essential that tests are never again used to judge schools.

To use a simple reading test, given one-on-one, compared with classroom assessments might be used for placement of a student in reading clubs only if those placements allow for immediate adjustments when the student is seen as progressing at a different rate. Clearly understand that tests are only a snapshot in time. Therefore, the teachers must confirm the grade level scores from their wide range of authentic classroom assessments. If there is a contradiction, that will be resolved in the placement as assessment is ongoing.

The Milwaukee Village School utilized the small, one-on-one test for initial placement in our Reading Clubs. In the Reading Club setting teachers then addressed the feasibility of the placement and made adjustments as necessary.

Although it is essential for students to improve at their best rate, to "catch up" to their peers becomes a "nonissue" as the new system does not allow for students to be compared to others. Education is not a race. That doesn't mean that there cannot be standards for informational purposes. It must be clear that those standards are simply guidelines for success, not deadlines for failure. And they are based on true assessment, not the test.

Consider this, first children blossom in different ways and at different rates. According to author Susan Ohanian, children learn like sap from a maple tree, one drip at a time. Of course, we want students to gain skills in a way that is natural to them. Students' skills, under this plan, will progress to their fullest extent. However, it must be in a way that is natural to the whole child. That is what students do when we trade winning for learning.

When you raise the bar for all students, school failure is assured. However, when you continuously raise the bar, ever so slightly, for the individual student, all will succeed but more important, all will learn. When students feel those individual gains, it is highly probable that the light bulb turned on and the student's level would continue to grow. Remember, in a race, to bring those students who are lagging behind up to level, they must learn faster than the better students. This is not a race.

When learning is taken out of the realm of politics and a wide range of assessments are used, then, and only then, will small individual tests have value as "jumping off spot" for specific purposes such as the Reading Clubs.

RECOGNIZING DIFFERENCES

The entire dynamic of the school is about to change. "Teach to the test" is no longer a consideration. This changes daily lessons dramatically. Teachers have their own design allowing more projects and innovative teaching. Simply put, teachers will take back their profession. Not only do class activities look different the atmosphere for learning is vastly improved. Not only does this bring back the joy of learning, but it also brings back the joy of teaching.

As we detail the complex approach to assessment, remember, we are replacing an ineffective single test with an assessment process that assures all children will have a quality education. It is difficult because educators throughout the years have preconceived notions about what a school should be. It is much easier to have students take a high stakes test and pretend that is achievement.

To hold schools accountable there must be a fair and honest assessment of that school. Every school has different students from diverse backgrounds with different abilities; however, there are essential fundamentals that can be documented and evaluated. As promised, I will repeat: Assessment is only as good as the information gathered and its application to the education of the child.

PARENTAL APPROVAL AND ACCESSIBILITY

Fundamental to any successful business is customer satisfaction. The same holds true for schools and should be included in a basic assessment. For this purpose, a satisfaction survey will be given to parents to provide their viewpoint on improving the school. This then becomes a tool of the overall assessment and accountability. It is extremely important that all parents respond to this survey. Often surveys are returned by more parents who have "successful" students and are comfortable with the school. Surveys of this type are not valid unless a wide range of parents respond.

An innovative way to assure every parent is included in the survey is to teach the students how to present that survey in a proper manner. This lesson analyzes the purpose behind surveys including how probability sampling is taken for a large population. Students will also learn how to verbally present the survey to parents who do not choose to do the paper version. This will allow students to understand the importance of parent surveys and why they should include 100% of the parent population if possible.

Training students to conduct surveys is not only an educational experience, but it is a lesson in democracy. A good experience is to visit a polling organization to see how they work. On many occasions where a large number of people attend, there would be someone standing with a clipboard looking for a particular person. One within a certain age group, gender, racial background, or whatever the polling was targeting. With the cooperation of the organization, have the students take the survey as well as give the survey to gain experience.

Once the survey is developed, have the students role play presenting the survey verbally. They may also role play the lead-in to the survey. A small script allows for consistency and validity to the survey. Here is an example: "Hello (family member). Will you be willing to complete a small survey? This particular survey will ask about your view of the new report card. Your views are very important to the school. Would you like me to ask you the questions or would you prefer to fill in the survey privately?"

An added advantage is that students will become closer to their parents. And the parents will trust their children giving the survey. These surveys are no longer filed away, never again to be seen. Upon implementation of the results, students report to classmates and parents how they were used as well as why the ultimate decisions were made. Their assessment is to successfully complete the survey of their parents and return it to school. Here is a small sampling of potential questions:

Parent Satisfaction Survey

- Has your child's teacher responded to your concerns?
- Have you been treated fairly by your child's teacher?
- Has the new school philosophy been explained to you?
- Do you feel school officials have listened to your concerns and ideas?

TEACHER SATISFACTION

Essential to implementing an effective school system is the ability for teachers to be able to teach and innovate at the highest level. With information from this survey, the school system will be altered to assure the full implementation of this new philosophy. If desired, this might be a confidential survey to assure all teachers' voices are heard. This, again, is a small sample. Make it your own!

Teacher Satisfaction Survey

- I have sufficient planning time.
- I have sufficient opportunity to participate in school development decisions.
- I have sufficient opportunities to attend external professional development events.
- Class size is sufficient to meet students' needs.
- I receive full cooperation from administration.

STUDENT SATISFACTION

The students play an integral part in the process of implementing the new philosophy. The time has come to become cognizant of the feelings of all students. Listening to them will allow many lessons to be learned. The students should make the decision whether to make this survey confidential. As with journaling, students rarely have a problem with the teacher reading their specific survey. However, if the surveys are anonymous, responses might be a more accurate sampling of the students' concerns. This is just another small sample of a student satisfaction survey:

- I feel teachers respect my feelings and opinions.
- I feel comfortable asking my teachers questions and discussing problems I am having in class.
- The kinds of things we do at this school and the way we learn makes me excited to come to school.
- Teachers talk with me about how I am doing in class and how I can improve.

GRADUATION RATES

It is easy to determine how many students graduate "on time" from a school. The focus now is on the number of students who graduate, regardless of time frames. The realization is that all children do not go through school at the same rate. Under this new innovative system, students could graduate earlier or later than the normal graduation date. The goal becomes for the student to leave the school on a path toward success, whenever that happens. Do you remember Roy? Success at age 20.

The question to be answered is this: of the students leaving the school, how many are graduating? Those are success stories. Those choosing to go to a different school may do so for many reasons. Some have moved to a different city. Some have sought another school for a specialty or other positive reasons. Dropouts are those who leave school without graduating and without enrolling in another school or program. Students remaining in a school are not considered a part of this equation until they graduate or leave the school.

The school is shown to be successful when students complete, or when it is verified that they continue toward their completion in another program. Schools are not penalized if they support every student. When a student leaves a school, that school must follow them until they connect with a proper program. This leaves no cracks for the students to fall through. If students drop into a program, they are not dropouts.

More information must be gathered for students who leave the school and why they leave the school. This information will become a part of the accountability measure of a school. Any student "dumped" to another school, no matter what the reason, will be surveyed, holding the original school accountable when appropriate. Again, if they legitimately drop into another program, they are not dropouts.

Particular attention must be given to those students who are removed from the school for behavior reasons. This new system takes into consideration the reality that for every student removed from the school by administration, a new student with the same or worse problems will replace them. The game of "whack a mole" must not continue. An exception to this is those who are dangerous to self and others. Of course, there are other special concerns but those are few and far between. A strong system of support must be in place for those students displaying problems. The team-building process is difficult, with every new student, it starts over.

This process is supported by the implementation of the MAP which follows students wherever they go.

SCHOOL ATMOSPHERE

Essential to the success of a school is an environment conducive to learning. The development of strategies at a fundamental level is designed to allow that environment to succeed. In addition to teacher, student, and parent surveys, the use of team-building activities will be a part of the school assessment.

Ongoing character development sessions, as previously described, keeps the students focus on issues that enhance their school and life experiences. In addition to surveys, the success of suspensions, accounting of the frequency and success of peer mediations as well as a visit to the school to determine the general atmosphere will be used to assess a quality environment. These activities and more will be considered along with their results.

- Compare the increase or decrease of an individual's suspension. Assess strategies used and their effectiveness.
- Dropout rates are compared to success rates such as graduation rates from the school or another school.
- Postsecondary success rates. This includes college and university placement, as well as special training placement and job placement. This is combined with a survey of student satisfaction with their placement.
- Attendance rates will be based on unexcused absences. Strategies to reduce this is also a consideration.

Students will be surveyed one year after graduation to determine their postsecondary successes such as job training programs, college or university placements, job placements, armed services, etc. Satisfaction with their placement will be considered. Note that it might not be possible to contact every student as they disperse throughout the world. That will be taken into consideration when determining success rates. If 100% of graduates cannot be reached, the data will serve as an estimate of the postsecondary success rate.

School environment will be determined as part of the student, parent, and teacher surveys as well as the above-listed issues. In addition, schools will be held accountable for the effectiveness of the strategies used. Strategies, by themselves, are not valid unless they are effective. Listed below are suggested strategies that will fit into the philosophy of the school. Again, make them your own, all schools are different.

- Nonviolent crisis intervention training prepares all teachers to deescalate a crisis.
- As a part of this new philosophy, all students are acknowledged for their successes.

- Students are welcomed into class on a consistent manner as part of a daily routine.
- A student behavior plan is created by a team of educators along with the student and parent, when necessary.
- Peer mediation is available with student mediators fully trained.
- Team-building activities for both staff and students are planned throughout the year.
- An active curriculum leads to class activities consistent with the new philosophy.
- Lessons flow smoothly as nonverbal communication, as well as other techniques, redirect students when needed.

Many of these activities are described elsewhere in this book. Add those you like to the list you have devised and seek out more ideas to assure successful students. There are also situations that are consistent with the philosophy that accidentally support a positive school atmosphere. As students leave the building on a regular basis, for community experiences, it is amazing how quiet the school becomes. Added to that an active curriculum and students are too busy being positive to be negative. Watch learning evolve where it is least expected.

A parent, while walking by a classroom of 12-year-old students, noticed essays posted on the wall for all to see. She suddenly burst into tears. Her son's work was there along with the rest. She had never seen her son write anything!

TEACHER SUPPORT

Assessment is only as good as the information gathered and its application to the support of the teacher. This quote will be adapted and repeated as many times as possible until it sinks in. Much is asked of the professional teacher. Much support must be available. To assure this availability, independent mentors will visit teachers in their classrooms on a regular basis. Initially, all teachers will be assessed. From the initial assessment, the teacher and mentor will decide future needs. Let the facts drive the support. These assessments are confidential between teacher and mentor. Of course, the teachers may share them if they choose.

STUDENT PROGRESS AS TEACHER SUPPORT

Any student progress on their demonstrated proficiencies will be between the teacher and mentor simply as informational. Never will assessments be based on a teacher test or a student standardized test score. Student progress on their proficiencies may be a "piece of the puzzle" to determine a teacher support plan by the mentor. This is a major part of the paradigm shift that is the result of the new system of education. Recognizing that assessment is for the purpose of supporting the teacher, confidentiality will be essential.

This is where unions enter the picture. They must support the fundamental purpose of assessment.

A student's past record of teacher's authentic assessments will allow progress to be charted to determine if the student had shown improvement on their MAP. As the MAP is individual, it is the student's progress that must move forward in a manner equal to or beyond that of past years. For example, if a student has made regular gains in their reading skills, and that progress had never been seen before, don't let anyone tell you that your school or the teachers are failures. If a child has made consistent gains in the past and is now floundering, teachers and mentors, possibly with the school psychologist and social worker will brainstorm ideas.

THE MANY CAUSES OF LOW STUDENT ACHIEVEMENT

This is a complex issue that will require critical thinking to determine the cause of the problem of low student achievement. It is never the teacher alone. Sometimes the power of the effects of poverty will override the best teachers. When low achievement is problematic in a particular student, action must be taken. Teachers teaming with counselors or social workers, for example, might need to visit homes of students to determine if anything has dramatically changed either there or in their neighborhood. Has there been any recent changes within the school environment? There are many more concerns to explore.

After all issues are considered, a full teacher assessment, by the mentor, may be necessary to determine if the teacher or team of teachers are using the quality strategies needed to support this student's success. For success, all assessments must be based on a wide variety of assessment tools. After several complete assessments over a period, the teacher will have opportunity to show growth and that will be extremely satisfying.

Teachers assessed and counseled were appreciative of the information gathered and growth was evident. For those who did not grow, many will work harder to succeed while some will realize they are in the wrong profession. It is the duty of a mentor to never give up on a teacher who is passionate about teaching. This new system will challenge every fiber of your being. It is not for the faint of heart.

Under this new system the teachers will be supported at every turn. The chaos of change is just that. It takes hard work and time to implement anything worthwhile. The solution is that no matter all the forces trying to reduce education to a single test, teachers must keep going forward and never give up. Do not forget that assessments are not given by, or even seen by administration. Small failures lead to large successes.

Systemic reform will require a small class size, sufficient planning time, and an assessment that is designed for support.

CLASS PREPARATION

Assessment consistent with this philosophy will support the teacher coming to every class prepared. A long-range plan connecting lesson plans to units and demonstrated proficiencies must lead in a specific direction to ensure student achievement. No longer will teachers follow the text verbatim. They will finally be allowed to become the professionals they were educated to be. Goals and objectives driving teacher expectations must be made clear. This may seem overwhelming however, it is what teachers do daily.

A well-planned class is essential to the new philosophy of the school. Even teachers with a wealth of experience will need a plan specific for the needs of the students. And these student needs may very well be different from the student needs of the previous years. For full support, mentors or assessors will access lesson plans as needed. For the support of the teachers, especially in the formative years of the new philosophy, the teaching units, lesson plans, and their connection to the student's MAP will be scrutinized.

Teachers will be provided with as much support as possible as the new philosophy is implemented, and beyond. Not only is this project essential for the success of all students, but it is also historical. Systemic change has been ignored for over 200 years. Catching up to today's needs is a major undertaking. Some may suggest that the change be taken one step at a time. The reality is once the dominoes begin to fall, there is no stopping them. You cannot eliminate letter grades without replacing them. The same with grade levels, and the "one size fits all" mentality.

Under this plan, administrative assessments will cover the areas of support after that full support has been given and/or will lead to additional support from the mentors. This will allow teachers to be fully supported on all levels.

QUALITY INDEPENDENT MENTORS

The mentors will be versed in the new philosophy. Activities such as community experiences and exhibitions will become second nature to the teachers with enough practice. Teachers will receive support in differentiated instruction, student-led projects, working with community partners, exhibitions, learning the value of questioning, and other important areas as defined by the new philosophy. As these mentors are completely independent from the school system and its administration, they will be nonthreatening to teachers. That is nonnegotiable.

Teaching strategies will be developed to fit into this new philosophy. Many of these strategies may already be in use by quality teachers on a regular basis. However, the new system creates an environment where innovation is vital to the success of the student and support is vital to the success of innovation. Quality teaching is congruous with quality support. Once the Target Schools are in place, those teachers will take the lead in developing additional schools and innovation will spread. This may seem like a lot to add to a teacher's list of strategies but think how many old worn-out strategies will be displaced. It will all fit in eventually.

EMBRACING DIVERSITY

One of the most important areas in education is to recognize the diverse backgrounds, environments, cultures, and learning styles that students possess. There will be many areas of education where groups of students will have a commonality. But areas that need special attention must be foremost in the minds of every teacher. This new philosophy is dependent on a focus on the needs of every student, excluding none.

Rather than a "one size fits all" philosophy of education, this new system recognizes that children grow and develop differently. The teacher must recognize the stages of development and adjust teaching accordingly. In the "one size fits all" philosophy, teachers were forced to spend much time judging, or even prejudging students. In some areas, students coming from a certain zip code are assumed to be behind and adjustments were made for those who were not. In this school, teachers will know where each student's skills lie. There will be no assuming.

Every teacher will be supported in their effort to provide students with a proper "jumping off point" for their learning process. No excuses!

As previously mentioned, the pre- and posttests will be given one-on-one at the school and compared to teacher classroom observations. Without politics and given by independent assessors like retired teachers, these tests now become part of an assessment and will give teachers a "jumping off spot" for the student lessons such as Reading Clubs. This takes some of the guessing out of placement levels. However, the test, as a snapshot in time, will lack accuracy. Under this philosophy there is absolutely no excuse for low expectations. Let the facts determine the "jumping off spot" and then the goals must be based on high expectations for every student.

Remember that the "jumping off spot" is step number one. Step two, adjusting the student placement, may happen almost immediately as there is no excuse for maintaining low expectations and low placements be they small groups or individual.

The difference is that this allows teachers to break away from the "one size fits all" philosophy and take students, following the MAP, on their pathway to success. Teachers will have support from mentors transitioning into the MAP philosophy. Educators will take ownership of the innovative philosophy and will continue to implement new ideas. The intention is to continually move forward to meet the needs of an ever-changing society.

Teachers will take on the challenge of abandoning past practices while moving forward to develop the new best practices. This will be historic!

Chapter 6

Straight Talk

The coronavirus pandemic has given us valuable information. Either we digest that information and take this opportunity to dive headfirst into systemic change or we cast it aside and continue the race to nowhere. In the words of Education Secretary Miguel Cardona, "If we think we are going back to how business is done before the pandemic, then we are missing an opportunity." The question is simple. Who matters? Who are schools for? In the past, schools have been designed for the elite. Thomas Jefferson said a school's purpose was to "rake a few geniuses from the rubbish." And some, in the eyes of the elite, didn't rise to the level of rubbish.

To use schools to "rank and sort" students to determine who goes to college and who struggles for work for the rest of their lives is unconscionable. That is what we have been doing for the past 200 years. It is always comfortable to take the easiest way, children be damned. This coronavirus crisis, however, has slapped us in our face with a wakeup call beyond anything in recent history.

No longer may educators and politicians ignore the needs of children only to take the easiest route. This was easily whitewashed in the past as these problems have existed for years. In the past and still occurring today, the victims were many Black and Brown students, the groups that our political leaders found advantageous to ignore. Never again!

Throughout the years an attempt to improve education by adding new ideas to a broken system has met with little or no success. Students are pushed out long before their time while many leave school lacking thinking and reasoning skills necessary to function in the world beyond the classroom. There is Sarah, a girl with special education needs, who left middle school, went to high school for three years, and dropped out. She still walked across the stage with a diploma. Moving forward without learning is not an option!

A teacher when asked if a student has been to class lately responded by saying "no, but don't worry, he will be sixteen soon. He'll drop out." This is not the norm for teachers, but it does exist way too often. Not only will we never again give up on children, but we will also approach all children in a respectful manner. Too many students are shuffled from school to school due to a preventable crisis. Under this new system and philosophy, even in a crisis, a protocol will be followed.

CRISIS INTERVENTION

Educators throughout the years have been prepared for any possible situation that may arise. Due to the rise in hate issues as well as the tension caused by the coronavirus crisis, the stress level of students as well as teachers and administrators is at an all-time high. As problems occur on a regular basis it is important that they are handled in a safe and secure manner by the school staff. This will reduce the stress level of students.

A school developed under the new system and philosophy of education will have nonnegotiables connected to its policies. The approach to crisis situations is high on that list. It is important to recognize the problems students face in the neighborhoods. More and more incidents escalate well beyond what is necessary. We begin with the approach educators might take to resolve problems at a variety of levels.

DEESCALATING A CRISIS

To begin we focus on the initial approach to a student whose actions are perceived as problematic. So how do we approach this situation without allowing it to escalate? Following the guidelines of nonviolent crisis intervention, the first step is to be supportive. To give the perception as well as the reality of being supportive it is important to relate to the students as well as their parents. Without that connection, the chances of escalation increase.

Always be respectful to every child. Never, ever embarrass a student in front of their peers. That will surely create a crisis.

A school staff member, connected to the student has a much better chance of deescalating the situation simply by talking it through. If the staff member bypasses step one and goes directly to step two, being directive, a confrontation is more likely. An example of what works is to approach the student of concern in a nonthreatening manner. The Crisis Prevention Institute (www.crisisprevention.com) teaches how to approach both verbally and physically. The initial conversation must be aimed at deescalating a potential crisis. Be patient and walk the person to a quiet location where the issue is discussed in a reasonable manner.

Here is an example of what not to do. A teacher was extremely angry at a student. They called for an administrator who arrived within seconds. The administrator deescalated the crisis and was walking the child to the office. However, the teacher followed, step by step shouting at the student. How long do you think it took for the child to calm down? You may respond in weeks, months, or years.

A child who has been abused at home will find any directive or punishment the school has to offer meaningless. In fact, they will invite abuse as that is their norm. The ultimate punishment for a child is to be physically abused by a parent. When confronted by a teacher, police officer, or the entire United States Army the response will be the same. That student will prepare himself to not only expect the worse but embrace it.

This has become the norm for that student, bringing with it an element of comfort. As in the situation above, the more shouting and demeaning that student, the more that student will prepare to take the challenge. The biggest mistake teachers, police officers, and other authority figures make when approaching a potential crisis is to start with step two and give a direct order. From there the escalation begins. Instead of deescalating a crisis, the crisis is escalated, not by the student but primarily by the teacher challenging the student.

No one knows whether individuals involved in crisis situations were abused at home, had mental illness, are in a crisis, or any other debilitating condition. Then, as the teacher in this example increases their verbal challenge, there is a good chance a physical confrontation will follow. Err on the side of caution. Assume the individual has issues, and begin with step one, supportive.

GOING TO THE NEXT STEP, DIRECTIVE

If at any time step one is not working, proceed to step two, directive. That is when you take charge of the situation and call for backup if needed. At this point, anything you do to avoid handling the situation alone is good. When support arrives, you have an additional set of eyes to observe and report the incident. More important, the other teacher can step in to mediate if necessary. A most difficult thing to do happens when a conflict occurs between the student and the first responding staff member. As help arrives, the first staff member must step back a goodly distance and a new staff member takes over. Often this will deescalate the situation.

A good example of this is to watch umpires in a Major League Baseball game. If one gets into a heated argument with a player or manager, another umpire will approach while the initial umpire will back off a significant distance. Major league umpires have it down to a science. There are those who see this supportive approach is weak, however, the reality is that it is humanizing. When we look past the outer shell into the inner soul, we see a human being. In many cases this approach will be effective. For more detailed information a good reference is the Crisis Prevention Institute.

> I have come to a frightening conclusion that I am the decisive element in the classroom. It's my personal approach that creates the climate. It's my daily mood that makes the weather. As a teacher, I possess a tremendous power to make a child's life miserable or joyous. I can be a tool of torture or an instrument of inspiration. I can humiliate or heal. In all situations, it is my response that decides whether a crisis will be escalated or deescalated, and a child humanized or dehumanized.—Haim G. Ginott

ABANDONING THE STATUS QUO

The shift from the 200-year-old system and philosophy of education to a new set of best practices will be difficult. The typical rhetoric will no longer work as the words will be analyzed, synthesized, and debated to discover what those worn-out statements really mean. It is time to begin the task of developing these new best practices. That begins with recognizing when deception is in play.

ABOLISHING GENERALIZATIONS

Begin this new system of education by throwing out generalizations commonly used by pundits and begin focusing on the facts. This is a primary function of the new philosophy. Not all children coming from an environment are the same. Let the facts determine where the "jumping off place" for a student's education is assigned. Use a small one-on-one test score combined with a teacher's classroom assessment as a snapshot in time to begin the student's pathway to success.

Whether it is believing everyone in poverty will have their learning negatively affected or that no one in poverty will, the system is ill equipped to serve all children in the way they learn best. Recognize that some children are fortunate enough to avoid the roadblocks of poverty. Those children are severely damaged by low expectations. Conversely, unrealistic expectations for those who are devastated by roadblocks such as childhood stress, malnutrition, drinking too much Flint, Michigan, water of the past, sleep deprivation, and racism, find the system's response is inadequate.

To resolve this problem and begin the process of developing a system that is on an even playing field, these realities must be acknowledged. Recognize the reality that roadblocks affect learning! It is especially important to remember the teacher has no idea who has roadblocks, and who does not. They must rely on facts based on high expectations for all students. That is why the small test, coupled with teacher observations must be ready immediately to find the "jumping off spot" for every student.

The days of guessing are over. Assessment must drive the curriculum and that assessment must be current. Zip codes only tell where to send the mail.

The systemic change presented herein dramatically changes the way we approach education. A structure of demonstrated proficiencies combined with authentic assessment brings students one step at a time along their pathway to success. A structure that treats failure as an integral segment of the learning process maintains students on that pathway. Generalized statements are replaced by facts that are clear to parents and educators alike.

Not only does this system teach children to never give up, but it also never gives up on children by failing them into oblivion or passing them without learning.

THE GAP

In the United States, we take a close look at general differences between Black and White students as well as Latinos. As we seek to walk away from generalizations, it is important to address problems with specifics. The Gap in learning is one of those issues. The current Gap is based on the artificial test scores that don't allow for the skills of the whole child. The Gap, currently, is a ploy to force students into second class achievement, where it is easier to create failures.

Warning! If you stop reading at this point you will miss the fundamental concept of the new system on issues like the Gap. Remember, the whole testing fiasco is based on the effort to keep a people down. What if students were assessed based on the whole child? To use the Gap to push children away from a complete education is unconscionable. However, to use it to place emphasis on those who are not progressing toward a learning goal that encompasses the whole child is essential.

The difference is, under this new system and philosophy the Gap is determined by progress toward learning goals and that also must be monitored for fairness. As a piece of the puzzle, the small pre- and posttest will be used to monitor the Gap as well. Gathering all the relative data will give a more specific view of achievement and a path forward to improving those skills. It is of utmost urgency that we develop an honest and accurate achievement level to respond immediately to those who are lagging behind.

We must be certain that one group of students is not being maintained at a lesser level of learning. The key word here is maintained. We must immediately recognize specific problems with specific students so those issues are immediately addressed. Every child is different so rather than focusing on the general statement that there is a Gap between races, we can use that generalization to focus on the children of a specific race who are lagging behind and can identify them and develop a plan of action to meet their specific needs. A strong focus on those specific needs must show progress.

The purpose of this change in the definition of the Gap is two-fold. First and foremost, to develop an honest assessment of students, not by the narrow scope of a single test but by the broad brush of an authentic assessment with a goal of determining the best way to teach. Second, there will continue to be a discussion of what group is lagging behind and why based on complete, whole child information with that generalization pointing to a specific definable need.

Under this philosophy, the need will be broken down to use as a "jumping off point" for the student's pathway to success. Earlier in the book it was made clear how a people were left behind. There were many reasons but all led to one generalization. That Black and Brown children are targeted and left behind. Now we will know which ones were the victims.

That generalization means nothing unless it points to specifics with a solution to the problem. The solution must be based on the genuine education of the whole child. Without that, the words are just political rhetoric. And so many people have as a primary language, the language of rhetoric. The language of rhetoric is driven by gross generalizations. Those gross generalizations must be recognized and deciphered to determine their real meaning.

ABANDONING THE COMFORT ZONE

Now be ready for more political rhetoric being directed your way. There is a whole system built upon letter grades and grade point averages. The elite are comfortable with the way things are. Many straight "A" students will become foot soldiers for those who want to maintain the status quo. They are happy with the abundance of praise heaped on them and the scholarships that follow. They do not want to lose all that glory just to be challenged by being pushed to the highest level of learning. That highest level is the level of failure.

Years back a middle school replaced the normal honor roll and honor classes that used grade point averages by Dr. Howard Gardner's Theory of

Multiple Intelligences. Those with skills such as Bodily-Kinesthetic; Spatial, Linguistic; Logical Mathematical; and more were and are considered intelligence. Of course, they didn't realize that Linguistic and Logical Mathematical could be traditional reading writing and arithmetic.

However, many saw bodily kinesthetic as simply basketball even though the range went from athlete to surgeon. Many parents were outraged as the honor roll as well as honors classes now included diversity. It took ten minutes for the local alderman to knock on the principal's door complaining. This exemplifies the effort that must be made to explain the details of the new philosophy as well as getting parents on board early. There will be many misunderstandings needing to be clarified.

Many realities must also be faced in the dramatic change brought about by this new philosophy.

The parents of the elite become elite themselves as their bumper stickers read "my child is an honor student at Colonel Ofcorn middle school." Of course, there is no thought to how those who are being pushed out of school feel. "They will drop out anyway." Right? Now consider the many elite universities who have an eye for the money as well as bragging rights if they can show their school is best. Universities are the best choice to lead innovation but that would not be in their interest.

Those universities get donations by saying their school is best and their school becomes best when they enroll academically elite students. They are comfortable with the elite being screened by the SAT and grade point averages. That is the easiest route. Those universities who are not considered elite are simply unmotivated to see anything change. It is much easier to look at grade point averages and SAT scores to determine whom to accept in their school.

Even a futile attempt to disguise the SAT exam with an "adversity score" assigned by the College Board was no more than shuffling the deck chairs on the Titanic. Simply giving points to students based on family income, environment, and educational differences, pigeon-holes the students based on generalities rather than the skills and abilities of the students themselves. Rarely, if ever would you hear a university chancellor say that a test score like the SAT is a predictor of success in a university! They know it is not. However, they do know the test score is the easiest way to accept students.

A university official once admitted that they gave less value to letter grades in urban areas than it did the suburbs.

DRAG THEM KICKING AND SCREAMING

A less than sincere apology must go to the College Board and their $1.1 billion revenue as well as a full apology to the 2.19 million students in 2020 who fell victim to the effort to be held hostage to an eighteenth-century school system. From this data it is easy to forecast the battle ahead. They will fight with every ounce of their energy to keep their status and money designed to do as much damage as possible to innovation as well as maintain the goal of Thomas Jefferson's day to rake a few geniuses from the rubbish.

They are in for a surprise because those who believe in all children, "aren't taking it anymore." The coronavirus crisis opened many eyes to the scam of the past. No longer will Black and Brown students be ignored for the sole purpose of the power, ego, and control of the College Board. In addition, look at the profits of the test prep companies with a value of $1.1 billion. They will not give up easily.

This is not to mention the ACT, PSAT/NMSQT, TOEFL, GMAT, IELTS, CAT, CLAT, B2 FIRST, and many more, possibly a whole alphabet worth of tests determined to keep the status quo with students frightened into purchasing every test prep available to be accepted at the best universities. These are powerful brainwashing tools to force students in their effort to maintain the subclass.

This will be the battle of the century to convince powerful businesses to go quietly into the night and give up those huge profits. The lobbyists will double their efforts to convince unwitting politicians to expend their political capital on this effort. The challenge is getting politicians to readjust their rhetoric. They are the ones most difficult to convince. They will lead the parade to maintain the status quo as they give simplistic answers to complex questions designed to bring donations in to fund their million-dollar campaigns.

"Competition will challenge all children to fight for the best test scores" they say. That will also take the focus off quality learning and into getting the best score at any cost. That is the main reason for cheating and the ultimate destruction of children is the result when they abandon learning for winning. In the new way of thinking, letter grades, grade point averages, honor roles, and the remainder of the caste system will disappear.

This new philosophy will be difficult for parents and children to comprehend. The challenge is to convert the thinking of students and parents alike to a focus on the true educational value of the portfolio. This will require the support of universities as they change their focus to information presented to them via that portfolio. There will be new needs in the educational world. Colleges and universities will need people to read and analyze the portfolios based on guidelines developed between those universities and the secondary schools as well as graduates and their parents.

In addition, teachers will need all the help they can get to develop questions that lead to a wide variety of subjects. All businesses are welcome to help as long as they understand that their ideas are not mandates. That the curriculum will be developed at the K–12 school level by a coalition of teachers, administrators, parents, and yes, even students. If businesses are willing to accept the new philosophy, they can learn to assist teachers rather than control them. If they can't make the change, they lose.

The chaos of change will be in full force requiring the educational community to bond together as one to maintain a strong focus on the new system and philosophy of education. Every effort will be made to drag the system back to what it was. Every trick in the book will be attempted and every political ploy will be a challenge. Since everyone has been in a school for years, everyone thinks they know how to run a school. They don't!

Would it really be too cumbersome for university personnel to read through a student's portfolio to realize what they really learned? Imagine accepting a student based on real information gathered throughout the student's high school career. Maybe a wide range of student information would be quite informative as an asset in guiding a student through a college career. The university system must be lobbied hard to assure not only that they understand the changes, but they can imagine how their university fits into the process.

> Do not just teach your children to read . . . teach them to question what they read. Teach them to question everything.—George Carlin

That statement by George Carlin was never more relevant than in today's political world. Simply put, do not believe anything! Research everything! As we battle for the souls of those students who need us the most, we must be aware of the strategies used to keep a people down. We start with the artificial test scores as they are generalized to mean the schools with the best scores make the best schools. That is the standard battle cry.

They then point to the schools serving the students who need us the most. Often those schools have their own battle cry. "But we serve those students from those zip codes, and they are damaged by poverty." These beliefs exist out of necessity. That is how the current system of education works. Yes, many of the students served have severe roadblocks in the way of learning. But not all.

FROM COMPETITION TO COLLABORATION

While the move is made from generalizations to facts, the move must also be made from competition to collaboration. The driving force behind the destruction of schools and the students in them is competition. Business CEOs talk about how great competition is. What they do not seem to know is schools are not building widgets. They are educating children who open or close their minds when they decide, not when the PR department decides.

Never again should politicians and administrators be allowed to push children out of school or cheat on test scores just to prove their school is best. Never again should children be pitted against each other for some to brag about being honor students while others hang their heads in shame. It is time to abandon the caste system design within public schools. Every child is important.

Under this new system there is plenty for everyone to be proud of. This simply means that success is celebrated wherever it falls. To be clear, competition is fine for a sporting event, a debate, an orchestra competition, or other similar activities. Learning to lose in those situations is healthy. No, we do not give everyone a medal. However, losing their education affects the rest of their lives. No longer will that be tolerated!

Instead of competing school versus school, it is time to ask the question, "whose children do you want to see fail?"

When a school has a great idea, and that idea works in the best interest of children, that idea should never be coveted. It should be shared for the educational world to utilize. It is not in the best interest of children for a school to make the best widgets. It is in the best interest of children for every good idea to be presented to the educational community. School competition leads to the ultimate destruction of children! The political elite are just so good at spewing out generalities. When collaboration upends competition, all children win!

If someone throws a generality at you, simply ask: what do you mean by that? Watch them squirm!

EMPOWERING TEACHERS

Empowering teachers to take back their profession is the most challenging change but also the most fun. It has been a long time since teachers have been heard in a way they deserve. Given that assessment is essential for professional growth and that quality assessment rarely happens under the current system of education, it is time to empower teachers to be a part of the process.

For those lucky enough to have a union, it might be a good time to collaborate with them along with a local university to redesign assessment to be a more highly valued tool.

Working in a team and within block time coupled with the concept that subject matter learning is not based on sitting time but on actual accomplishments allows great flexibility. In this block of time, teachers are able to create groupings that best fit the learning styles of the students. That leaves open many possibilities that are totally owned by the teacher. They decide time frames, within the block, for every activity. There are no rules regarding sitting time and the subject matter will relate directly to the students MAP, as the teachers decide. The empowerment of teachers to teach is the most invigorating aspect of the profession.

Never again will teachers want to go back to the old way of teaching.

LET THE CHANGE BEGIN

If systemic change is to exist, a broad base of support must be established. Begin with the parents and the use of surveys as earlier described in this book. To gather information from a wide variety of parents will help give direction to a new school system. The goal here is not necessarily to get advice but to identify problems and concerns. Which concerns are not addressed in the old system and which concerns are addressed but are not effectively resolved? This will give a base from which to start the process. The gathering and analyzing of information are essential to developing a plan of action.

"For support, go to the neighborhood, knock on doors, and talk to the invested community members, the parents whose children will attend your school."

Connections must also be made with community members and businesses who will not hesitate to describe their needs that remain unfulfilled. It is important to focus on gathering information. Presenting to parents on the first day of the new school, teachers decided to give the cookie assessment. This all started on a warm summer's evening what seems like centuries ago.

> As a new community school, we watched parents approaching from blocks away, walking to their child's new school. Flyers were sent, calls were made and doors were knocked on and Bar B Que Chicken Wings were ordered so parents could dispense with their evening meal and attend the meeting. Families started showing up slowly and continued until we had a full house. Families not only included the parents and the new students, but any other siblings, cousins or grandparents who choose to learn about the school.

This was the student's first time in school so three teachers took them into another room while we presented our innovative ideas to a receptive audience. For the students presentation, they were to develop a "cookie assessment" that we learned at Alverno College. The students were given three kinds of cookies to assess, with one group giving the cookies a letter grade and another group giving a short description of the cookies.

The first team averaged an "A" grade for the cookie but no one could guess what kind of cookie it was. Angela gave her summary of the cookies they had. "It was a small round cookie with cookie dough, sugar and pieces of chocolate in it." What a surprise, everyone guessed it right. And that was used as proof to parents why we didn't give letter grades. Since they don't say anything constructive, they could easily be used to cover up what the child hasn't learned.

When asking for advice there will be more responses than can be imagined. Most of those responses will be based on individual backgrounds in an out-of-date dysfunctional school system. "I like the old school philosophy and I turned out OK." But did everyone turn out OK? Not likely! Once fundamental information is gathered, the effort must be made to gather educators of kindred minds to form the basis of a new school. This is difficult for many reasons.

Many can talk the talk but when the rubber hits the pavement, they slide back into the old system. The system they know and are comfortable with. All it takes is a couple saboteurs to slow the process or destroy it. And those are the ones who had to be convinced. The ones who hid behind letter grades so that parents wouldn't know what their children accomplished. The ones who will never really know what that cookie is.

ADDRESSING MURPHY'S LAW

Remember Murphy's Law, "anything that can go wrong, will." The effort will take time to develop, and an early start is essential to deal with those things that go wrong. In a school with the traditional schedule of several months off in the summer, the entire summer must be fully staffed to have proper time to prepare. As the saying goes "The first 90% of the project will take 90% of the time and the last 10% of the project will take the other 90% of the time." Yes, you read that right.

Systemic change will be met with many obstacles. Some of those might be roadblocks set up by self-appointed community leaders who have their own agendas. They will have a strong networking system well established. Do not be surprised if their ideas go all the way to the governor. "Murphy's Law" will be widely in force as every political agenda known to mankind and woman kind will be on full display. The book co-authored by Eldon Lee and Mary Gale Budzisz entitled *Quashing the Rhetoric of Reform* (Rowman and Littlefield) offers a more detailed list of the hits we took developing the Milwaukee Village School years back.

DESIGNING TARGET SCHOOLS

How should consultants be utilized to support the school developing process? Every public school has professional educators on staff. Not everyone has the experience to develop an innovative school. A "Target School" may be utilized to bring in those innovative teachers and support staff that not only will be interested in developing a model but will be passionate about it. With that effort and the reading of this book and others, consultants should not be necessary.

As the program evolves and the need spreads to other schools, those who developed the "Target Schools" will become the consultants. Remember, under this new system, "best practices" have not been developed yet. Will unions be on board for this "radical" change? Pay attention to leaders such as Randi Weingarten of the American Federation of Teachers, AFL-CIO, as she speaks about the needs of children: "kids need time for problem solving, critical thinking, applying knowledge through project-based instruction, working in teams, falling down and getting right back up to figure out what they didn't understand and why."

Throughout the startup of a new system and philosophy there will be every attempt to drag back to the comfortable system everyone is familiar with. In the beginning the United States Department of Education along with that department in every state must collaborate to provide consistency. It will be no surprise if some states don't comply. Then it is necessary to partner with those states that do.

The stage is set, the players in place. It is time to act. There is much at stake that will require a great deal of energy and perseverance. Pull your teams together and start making plans today. Not one minute should go by depending on the outdated system of education. With the problems caused by the coronavirus crisis, a wide variety of skills are scattered all over the board. Just remember, Who Matters? And move ahead.

BUILDING THE TARGET SCHOOL

Developing a proposal for a new school takes hours of research, knocking on doors, and brainstorming ideas. Begin by gathering a wide variety of educators, community activists, business leaders, neighbors, and other influential people of kindred minds. Seek out those with a wide variety of experiences that will not only be creative but will also challenge your thinking. As you move ahead, those creative thoughts will be a wakeup call for those committee members.

A committee could be composed of a personnel director of a major corporation, a nurse, university professor of special education, judges, lawyers, politicians, block clubs, union, parents, students, and anyone who will add to the conversation in a positive way. Diversity is a top priority. Remember, this committee is not designed for appearance. It is designed to get information from a wide variety of sources.

When gathering this committee, force yourself on those who are innovative and have influence. And don't take no for an answer. You would be surprised how many appreciate that if they are really for children. You are going to need it when the rest of the world is dragging your school back to the old way of thinking. Select your committee carefully because the saboteurs are everywhere.

THE CHAOS OF CHANGE

"Posing a threat to the central office power base, a new innovative school will be targeted, and the resolve of its staff challenged in ways that reach beyond imagination. However, if you keep pounding away at good ideas, and those ideas are logical and show success, systemic change will follow."

As you develop the basic structure and design of the school, seek guidelines from the State Department of Education personnel and others who are designated to approve the school. The goal of the committee is to develop a plan to implement the new philosophy within the school. However, the new philosophy must allow the empowerment of the local school as long as that school does not revert to the old ways. Fundamental to the new philosophy is that it is designed to serve all children on an even playing field.

Upon preparing the proposal, take it door to door to the parents of the students who will most likely attend. This is convenient in a neighborhood school as those parents will be easily accessible. Listen to their opinions, not of one or two parents but as many as you can muster. Be sure the process is started well in advance of the target opening date of the new school. In a typical school year, this proposal should be completed by the end of the previous school year thus allowing the entire summer (or designated vacation time) to hire and work with educational staff.

Once teachers and other support staff are hired, implementation of the school philosophy will begin. Regardless of curriculum coming from other entities, it is important to develop your own. Remember, the curriculum is not based on sitting time, it is based on completing the requirements the school has developed. The goals, as led by the MAP, is the guiding factor in curriculum planning. First begin with broad categories:

- Communication Skills
  - Reading
  - Writing
  - Speaking
  - Listening
  - Signing
  - Languages
  - Performing Arts
- Problem Solving and Analytical Thinking
- Physical and Emotional Wellness
- Community Awareness
- Professional Preparation
- Technology

Notice the flexibility of "Communication Skills" in this sample. Yes, the arts are included as communication skills because that is what they are. You can include anything that will support the child's future beyond the classroom. As goals are set within these categories, we are reminded that they are not Common Core goals where the result might be pass or fail. These are demonstrated guidelines for success specific to a student's MAP. Although many goals will fit most students' MAP, they may not fit the same time frames.

Planning for a process to meet all students' time frames will take a good deal of creativity. However, if minds are open to an array of available times, regardless of former rules and regulations, the process will succeed. Unions are a good partner to have in this effort. The approach should not ask if the school design fits into union, management contracts. Make the process meet the needs of children and then ask how to fit it into a contract or how the contract could be altered to fit the school.

As you work with the whole staff, hired three months before the start of school, start with generalities and immediately go to the specifics of the curriculum as well as the infrastructure of the educational process. The importance of the curriculum is to embrace a wide range of knowledge. Never, ever let the textbook companies determine the curriculum. To accomplish this a wide range of websites and books must be made available to students. Research is essential to the new philosophy.

The arguments about what should be taught in school have gotten out of hand. Simply ask students to research an issue. That research will lead to a gold mine of information, chosen by students. Let research fall where it falls.

Students should never simply accept the textbook companies' view of the world. They should question, analyze, debate, and come to conclusions. That is where the resources must be made available. There are so many questions to answer as you prepare for the opening of the school. Take each innovation, one by one and determine how to implement it. Here are some sample questions to get you started.

- How and where will the exhibitions be held?
- What space is available as we separate students in our team?
- When and how will you prepare students to meet proficiency if they are not immediately successful?
- What will the student MAP look like?
- How will you help students understand their MAP?
- What will the "report card" look like with no letter grades?
- With no schedule during block time, what are the many ways to utilize that time?
- How will you integrate the curriculum to serve the needs of all?
- What will a portfolio look like?

You will develop many more issues to be worked out before the start of school. Now you understand the importance of planning time. It is essential for a professional teacher to be able to apply their craft. Only through quality planning time will this happen. Keep in mind there will be those who will want to program you for failure. Here are some nonnegotiables. Make them your own by adding or subtracting issues.

- There will be no "teach to the test" curriculum.
- There will be no high stakes standardized test given.
- No written chapter tests.
- No textbooks to guide the curriculum. (Some may be used as resources)
- Never give letter grades.
- Never retain a student as grade levels are no longer an indication of achievement.

Again, make these your own. Take what you like, throw out what you don't. It is your school, and the system and philosophy must be yours. As you develop your new school, keep in mind there is no time to waste. We have already wasted centuries. The coronavirus crisis has magnified the needs of students. The realization is that students who miss a year or more of school will be diminished in the caste system called school. This is added on to those who have already been diminished due to a wide variety of issues.

There is hope in the future though as the United States Department of Education seems to be gaining the foresight to recognize the systemic problems with education. The action must begin by those in the trenches. As the Education Department begins the action from the top down, you, in the classroom, begin the action from the trenches up. Hopefully, when you meet, the system and philosophy of education will be replaced.

"If not now, when?"—Hillel the Elder

Chapter 7

Help Is on the Way

The development of a new system and philosophy of education will be the most difficult task ever attempted by mere mortals. The opposition will be antagonistic, willing to fight to the end to save their positions of power. The textbook companies will hire more lobbyists to swarm on Capitol Hill, convincing that the good old days were good after all. And politicians will bow to the textbook companies with their generalized rhetoric.

CONFRONTING OUR FEARS

Remember the part of the book that talks about striking fear into others for political purposes? Be ready, because here it comes. In addition to those trying to control the minds of children, there are others who just want better schools as long as they aren't different. And then there are those who are stuck in a rut. They are just happy with the way things are. Joe Garba, former Dean of Education. Hamlin University:

> I often think that while almost everyone wants our schools to be better, almost nobody wants them to be different. But I really don't believe we can have the kind of schools we need in the 21st century if we aren't willing to make them significantly different from the school's we had in the 20th century. And I don't believe we can get the kind of schools we need by changing the ones we've got.

That is exactly why this book is not about *fixing* a failed system of education, it is about *replacing* it. But how will it be replaced? Of course, the charter school advocates will be on their megaphones shouting to the world that if we only change the name of schools and get them away from the current public system, we can do the job. How has that worked for them so far?

Rare has the charter school displayed innovation, rather they have served a warmed up version of the same philosophy. Just look at their test scores they say. There is no denying the possibility of creative ideas happening in charter and other schools, but will they last? So many have fallen for a variety of reasons and others, said to succeed, have good test scores but lack substance. They shout from the mountain tops, "All my students went to college and they were all from poverty homes."

PUTTING ON THE FLAK JACKET

Remember the discussion about students in poverty and those who have been sheltered from the overpowering obstacles? Which poverty children does your school serve? Their hope is that the people they are shouting at, have the racist belief that all Black children, in poverty are the same, and their school saved them. "But we were fair as all our children were chosen by a lottery." Do all parents apply through the lottery or are they simply the elite? So many questions, so little answers. When some educators shout that all their children are from single parent homes, is that not disrespectful of those powerful single parents who raise great kids?

Although this will be the toughest job any teacher has undertaken, it will change history! Even more powerful, it will change the lives of so many young people, for the better. Hope will prevail if all teachers bond together with parents and other people of kindred minds and stay on message. Do not get distracted with the rhetoric of the past. It will come at you in waves, one after another.

Remember it took 200 years of hard work to create an elitist system, replacing it will be a long tedious process. The "jumping off point" begins as Target Schools are developed in the image of the dreams presented in this book as well as others. Take a look at the works of Deborah Meier in New York City, and in Boston where the dreams live on. It is now time to dive through the window of success as it opens, just a crack and develop a Mission Hills School or a Milwaukee Village School or a Central Park East school in every state in the union.

The trick is to stay under the radar. As much as it is the nature of great educators to share creative ideas, now is the time to be sneaking and conniving for the good of the students who need us so desperately. So when we jump through that window of opportunity, make sure we land quietly on a soft pillow. Then, when it is complete, we share it. A small number of Target Schools are recommended so we don't scare the Standardistos.

Imagine the look on the faces of educators as they ponder the possibility of a school empowering teachers. Feel the enthusiasm build at the prospect of innovation that will allow teachers to serve all students in the way they learn best. There is excitement for the chance to never again give a fake letter grade. No longer will they have to struggle to force academic drivel down the throats of unsuspecting youth. To never again have to struggle with the ongoing questions that have no answers under the current system of education.

Never again will these teachers have to decide whether to promote someone lagging behind or fail them into oblivion. Teachers will no longer be concerned by unfair judgments of teachers and students alike, based on students' standardized test scores. And never again will they be given a script for a teach-to-the-test curriculum. In other words, teachers will be able to take back their profession. Such joy on the face of teachers until one quiet teacher, in the back of the room says, "How can we do all these innovations all by ourselves?"

LOOKING FOR HELP

The room gets quiet. "What if we don't get planning time or small class size. How can we do this all by ourselves?" The answer is simple, you can't! The first goal is to get planning time and small class size and that will take a great deal of political capital. Some administrators will see the importance of these changes and build a budget around them. Others will refuse to give up power and keep their teachers controlled by yet another test and overwhelmed by classes way too large to function, thus creating another way to blame teachers.

When there is a window of opportunity, you must not just jump through it, you must dive head-first into it. However, there must be a strategy that will allow the process to move forward one step at a time. That one step must be part of a sprint to implement the greatest advance in the history of education. This change is the stuff from which heroes are made. Who among you has the courage to take the challenge?

WE CAN'T DO IT ALONE!

When we talk about giving students a second shot at proficiency or the exploratory workshops the discussion leads to time frames and how they will fit in. For students there is time after school, before school, on weekends, and designated vacations. However, for teachers, there are only a limited number of hours in a week. With that in mind, it is important to utilize the entire community in the process of learning.

The coronavirus crisis, as well as the realization that many students have been in a crisis for centuries, leads to a discussion of the value of the Community Learning Center. Never has this concept been so important. The 21st Century Community Learning Center is a federally funded program supported by state Departments of Education for out-of-school-time programs, which include those before school, after school, or in the summer.

The intent of learning centers in general is to bring the community businesses and support agencies into the school to serve the students. The school provides the facility and the students while the CLC (Community Learning Center) manages the program providing needed services. This manager is often a not-for-profit organization such as a Boys and Girls Club, The YMCA, a church, or any other not-for-profit program chosen by a local committee to serve children. As the CLC is not managed by the school even religious groups may apply.

One ideal example of cooperation between business and education is when a fitness center was brought into the program. They offered fitness classes for the elderly for $1.00 each within the school, after the school day is over. Thus, the elders in the community are supported for a reasonable cost and they are brought into the school not only to utilize a vacant facility but to bring the elders closer to other support services available in the center. So many support services, all within a community, is essential to the wide range of community members. Think of the possibilities that would enhance the health and safety of the neighborhood.

- Supporting expecting moms.
- A childcare center.
- A clothing exchange.
- A visiting dentist for students and neighborhood adults.
- Visits by specialists such as foot care, diabetes care, blood pressure checks, etc.
- Connecting elders to a service.
- Fitness classes.

Imagine these elders leaving their fitness classes and spending two hours a day working with young children, reading stories to them. Modeling reading to young children is a great beginning to their joy of reading. Reading, however, is only one of many ways to use the experience of the elderly. What if you have a retired accountant, lawyer, or someone who lived through the Depression? Think about a history lesson when it leads to a real-time experience.

What was it like driving that 1948 Studebaker with no seat belts, no radio, no power steering, and so many dying in car accidents, the list goes on. Every year a great experience goes away as the elders pass the baton to another generation. At this writing, there are those who remember celebrating Hitler's birthday in Germany and being bombed out of their homes. They remember running across the fields to escape the abuse of Russian troops or walking miles to get to the safe part of Berlin. And they remember escaping to the United States seeking freedom and safety.

The list goes on as these 80-and 90-year-old elders share their stories and experience perhaps at one station of 15 students or an assembly of 1500. Think of the occupations of those elders as they exercise in the CLC, that exists right down the hall in the same school building as the classes. There is a wealth of history in the elders, and they are right at the school's doorstep, just waiting to be asked.

The stories of a retired spy like Valerie Plame, a civil rights leader like Rev. Jesse Jackson, an astronaut like Joe Acaba, a nurse, a politician, and a farmer would capture the interest of all. That list goes on and on. Whether they are famous or everyday citizens, they all have a story to tell. Those stories are a piece of history, but they are fading fast as elders do not live forever. Bringing those experiences to life would enthrall your students as well as the elders who love to tell their stories.

- Academic enrichment programs, such as proficiency guidance.
- Hands on science, technology support, and exploratory workshops.
- Community service opportunities, a great support for the new system.
- Mentoring, helping those who are showing a potential for problems like violence.
- Education by professionals in the community.
- Music: Wouldn't it be great if students could compose songs here?
- Sports: The best of the team-building process.
- Arts: could include art therapy for those who would benefit from it.
- Cultural activities, to allow students to dream.
- Other activities designed to support the new curriculum.

The vision presented in this book is to utilize the CLC as a support system for the students. The CLC, utilizing the services of community businesses and industry, could easily develop exploratory workshops related to a specific profession. Remember, these workshops are available to all students regardless of skills and are designed to give those students an overview of a specific skill area. Who better to do this than professionals in the field?

The CLC could also be available to those who did not meet proficiency in a specific area. The student having difficulty with a budget-related math project would welcome support from an accountant from a local firm. A specialist could work with a small group of students after school, on a weekend, or whenever available until they achieve proficiency. The ideas are endless if we just look for them.

UTILIZING THE PARTNERS

Let your imagination go wild. Imagine the CLC housing a health center that is available for all parents, neighbors, and students. In these trying times that is essential for the health and welfare of all. In addition, they can serve many functions. Dalvery Blackwell, of the Tobacco Free Task Force in Milwaukee, describes her experiences with students planning an antitobacco conference called the TKO. Dalvery worked for the Village School business partner The Black Health Coalition:

> The whole concept of the conference was peer to peer education. It allowed the youth to lead us in developing this whole concept. It was their idea, it was initiated by them, it was created by them. We had a two month training session every Saturday, we had students from four different schools, four different ethnic groups where they learned about the tobacco industry's deceptive advertising tactics, they learned about the health risks of smoking and they also learned leadership skills and how to conduct an effective workshop.
>
> I'm still working with tobacco control initiatives with the Black Health Coalition, I was just meeting with the Wisconsin Tobacco Board last week in Madison (WI) and several people came up to me and said, Dalvery, since that time we have not seen anything yet comparable to the TKO conference . . . we do have a tobacco prevention center, now, as a result of all the work that took place four years ago.

In addition, a variety of health organizations helped with a health fair and recommended healthy snacks to sell at a small store within the school. In these days of dis-information, organizations like the Black Health Coalition are essential to the complete education of your students. Beyond thinking past the confirmation bias, bringing experts in to present accurate information is a necessity.

One way to assure accurate information getting to students and parents alike is through a health fair. There you can provide a variety of professionals to respond to student questions and concerns. Students can prepare the toughest questions they can find and seek a variety of answers from professionals from their neighborhood. The more they are familiar with the professional, the more they would trust their responses.

Think about the questionable statements made in this day. Can students separate fact from fiction? Can they separate half-truths from total truth? To assure trust, have the students, under the guidance of a health professional organization select the presenters from a list of quality professionals. Think about some of the current issues in this day of the coronavirus crisis. Detailing the problem allows educators to understand why there is an extreme difference in people's beliefs. Stated another way, a little bit of knowledge can do a whole lot of damage.

During the health fair, these issues can be brought to light without using opinions, by just using the facts. Let the students draw their own conclusion and defend them. Questions will come from all student levels, not only for the professionals but children can also question the opinions of their parents. Along with health professionals and organizations, a wide variety of information will be made available to students. And the teacher can step back, except to lead the discussion. The less educators express their opinion, the more learning process is trusted.

Business partners have been discussed throughout this book. They are an essential part of the new philosophy. The Readers Choice Bookstore owner, Carla Allison, partnered with the Village School Book Club. From that experience, she connected with other schools to start a book club. Locally owned D&L bus company owned by David and Sarah Crouthers took our students everywhere from a local garden to Boston. All in a coach, not the yellow school bus. CH2MHill partnered with our water purification project, while MATA media brought our students into their television studio for a project. Vel Wiley was the director at MATA Media:

> It was through the success of you young ladies and many other students that (teacher) Mary Gale Budzisz brought through that really led to our ability to get a grant and create a formal educational access department.—Vel Wiley to MVS students Chante and April.

How many projects light a spark that creates more access to learning? Every organization you partner with may easily lead to more experiences for a wide range of students. Our students were regular visitors to Will Allen's Growing Power to learn the wide range of skills needed to be a farmer and more. Will expanded his organization to include people of all ages interested in urban farming. He was named one of TIME magazine's 100 Most Influential People.

As you develop your school, start bringing in your partners early in the process. It is amazing how many businesses will jump at the chance to help your students. And they will enjoy it as much as the children. Remember, you can't do it alone, nor is it necessary. Partners are everywhere with a wide range of skills just waiting to help. At Village School we never got turned down by a business.

THE PARENT CONNECTION

A community school is necessary to keep a strong connection with parents. A community school is a school where children walk to school, parents have access to school without driving across town, and educators can easily connect with families. Where parent meetings are also neighborhood meetings. Parents must again be guiding lights of a school designed for children and never again take a back seat in the educational direction of the school.

SECURING THE ROLE OF PARENTS

There are some things parents can do and some they can't, but their voice must be heard regardless. Often parent committees are designed for appearances rather than for substance. Some schools insist that 51% of a committee be parents. Although this may sound good, those parents only speak for themselves. There is a false belief that a parent on a committee can speak for all the parents of all the students. Often those parents on the committee speak for themselves only or are forced to be puppets for the administration. Often, they will be recipients of a smile and a nod followed by being completely ignored as in this true story:

> The Milwaukee Village School had an agreement that when it came time to hire a new administrator, the parents would have a strong voice. When the administrator retired, the central administration came and hired a new one who had no knowledge of the innovative philosophy of the school. The parents had no say in the matter even though they wanted someone who would carry on the philosophy. The school closed in shambles a couple of years thereafter. It is time for the parents to have their say, especially in the goals of the school.

Here is what it looks like when parents are consulted. The question of dismissal time for the school came up:

> As the middle school students were housed in a building along with high school students, the administrator thought it best that they be dismissed at different times to avoid conflicts. A poll was taken of all parents and the response was overwhelmingly in favor of the two schools being released together. When asked why, parents responded that their children have brothers and cousins in the high school to walk home with them. Although the ultimate decision was that of the school administrator, the students were released together that year.

EMPOWERING PARENTS

This new parent committee will be charged with the responsibility of hearing all parents. In the new philosophy, they will survey all parents, using the students to present the poll to their parents as assurance that all parents voices will be respected. They will then work with administration especially in the area of goal setting. No longer will parents be confined to planning homecoming, school dances, and bake sales.

They will be especially involved in the goals of the school and kept informed on all issues. Their voices will no longer be trivialized. Every parent in every corner of the school district will be respected and their voices heard. That includes the parent who had a tough time in school and is struggling with everyday life. The one who has no desire to come anywhere near the school. Every parent means every parent!

Although the hiring of staff must be in the hands of administration, when that staff might influence the overall goals of the school, parental voices must be heard. The fundamental direction of the school is at stake and a simple change in personnel might either reinforce that direction or sabotage it. As the parents are fully involved in goal setting, administrators must see to it that the policies of any new personnel are consistent with the school philosophy.

The power of the parents negates the power, ego, and control of central office and school boards if utilized properly. Begin welcoming all parents by inviting them to a meeting before the beginning of the school year. Be sure to make it convenient for them. It is difficult for parents to work, come home, and cook for the family and then run off to a meeting. Taking one of those issues off the table, a catered meal was always provided, and all family members welcomed. The power of neighborhood has many twists and turns. It can start with crisis and end well or start well and end with a crisis. Here's a story about Mary and Jan. Of course, not their real names:

Mary and Jan came to school one day ready to demolish each other. Shouting and screaming could be heard for miles. When an administrator showed up at the scene the shouting stopped and fists flew confirming that students are more likely to fight when someone shows up to stop them. An attempt at mediation was failing so it was decided to send them home separately for one day to cool off.

An hour later Mary showed up with six people she described as relatives. They did not appear to be here to talk. As soon as they were convinced that Jan wasn't at school, here she comes with her family and friends seemingly to resolved the matter. After a long conversation, the families were convinced to leave if one parent for each student would stay to discuss the matter.

At the conference they talked and the administrator mediated for almost two hours. During that time valuable information was gathered. The fact that the whole difficulty was based on "he said, she said" became trivial in the face of the knowledge that these parents lived two blocks from each other and have never met. It was time to introduce these neighbors to each other.

Due to easy access to the school these parents met, exchanged phone numbers, share hugs, and now help each other look out for their children. They even have backyard barbecues together. It is valuable to go back to olden days when, if children mess up on the other side of town, the parent is waiting for them when they get home, and it better be before the streetlights turn on.

THE TRUTH IS IN THE DETAILS

Due to the problems caused by generalizations, it becomes important for students to look at the details whenever looking for in-depth answers. This is long but it will give educators an idea of how and why to have students break down the details before making decisions. It is not the role of the school to tell students the results, it is the role of the students to research, analyze, synthesize, debate, and try to come to a conclusion. Even if they can't agree on a conclusion, it is still important for them to reach their conclusion and try to justify it.

According to a scientific study by the Environmental Protection Agency collaborating with the University of North Carolina, April 5, 2021, (EPA Researchers Test Effectiveness of Face Masks, Disinfection Methods Against COVID-19) researchers tested how well different masks and modifications filter out airborne salt particles, which are the same size as the smallest SARS-CoV-2 particles. "We've performed hundreds of tests to provide the most useful information for decision makers and the public to help fight this virus," Dr James Samet, research biologist on the project. Here are some results of that study. This is a great project for high school students and even middle school. How about adapting it for elementary students?

> The researchers examined the filtration ability of a variety of medical procedure masks, cloth masks and coverings recommended for the public. They tested masks made from cotton, nylon, and other materials and in different styles, including masks with ear loops and ties. They found that the effectiveness of the masks varied widely: a three-layer knitted cotton mask blocked an average of 26.5 percent of particles in the chamber, while a washed, two-layer woven nylon mask with a filter insert and metal nose bridge blocked 79 percent of particles on average. Other masks scored somewhere in between.

They also tested a variety of modifications to improve the fit of commercially available medical procedure masks, like tightening ear loops, placing rubber bands over the top and bottom of the mask to reduce gaps, and placing a cut-out piece of nylon stocking over the mask to seal the gaps. The filtration ability improved by 60.3 to 80.2 percent depending on the modification made. As the fit of the medical procedure masks improved, so did their filtration efficiency. . . .

In their study of masks recommended for the public, the researchers emphasize the importance of mask material and fit. Their results indicate that not only are certain cloth masks effective at keeping out viral particles, but in many cases perform as well as or better than non-N95 medical masks. Fabrics with multiple woven layers and reducing gaps provide substantially more particle filtration.

The team continues to explore mask performance with studies in progress on the effects of facial hair and face shape on mask fit. The results of these projects will help the public and health care professionals choose mask options that provide the greatest level of protection. Everyone should be aware of the effort to create the best mask possible in this day of ongoing pandemics.

The purpose of presenting this detailed information in this book, is to demonstrate how bits and pieces can be extracted to fit every point of view. The three-layer knitted cotton mask did let 73.5% of small particles through, thus supporting the view of some that those tiny particles go right through the mask. However, the two-layer nylon mask only let 21.5% through while blocking 79.5% of the particles.

If, as a teacher, you simply say masks work and a parent counters by saying they do not, the discussion must not end there. Have students read, at least, the summary of the study for middle schoolers and the whole study for high schoolers. Research, analyze, debate, and then come to a conclusion. Actually, this study could be simplified for elementary students by bringing in samples of a wide range of masks and showing the proper way to wear them.

STAYING SAFE IN TRYING TIMES

"It takes a village to raise a child" is an African proverb that means an entire community of people must interact with children for those children to grow in a safe and healthy environment. As we have learned from the coronavirus crisis, keeping children healthy is a full-time job. Add to that, the issue of safety leaves our head spinning trying to think about ways to accomplish that without superhuman strength.

Superhuman strength, of course, is only in the movies so it is time to strategize. No one can do it alone, but together great achievements can be accomplished. First there must be an effort to recognize and anticipate potential problems. If you can circumvent a crisis, a disaster can be avoided. Here we look to neighbors and local businesses to help by protecting our children.

DEVELOPING SAFE PATHS

Educators, as well as parents should receive training on how to spot "red flags" when they show up in conversations as well as on the internet. See something, say something is the slogan, however there is more value to that statement when they know what to look for. It is time for those who have knowledge, share it, no matter how minor it seems.

In a neighborhood where students walk to school, it is valuable to establish a safe way home for all. Of course, there are school crossing guards throughout communities. Here are some thoughts for those who feel more support is needed. Safe paths are a way to provide security to those who have concerns about their child walking home from school. This is important to a neighborhood school as safety is a major concern when parents choose a school for their children. Begin by putting a map of the wall with pins indicating where students live. From that, locate the major streets that lead to the school.

The next step is to locate families or businesses along the safe path routes. Once they know the arrival and dismissal times of the students, they are asked to step out on the porch to keep an eye on the students. They all have the phone number of the school to contact if necessary. In addition, to ensure safety, a staff member from the school will monitor those paths. In a neighborhood school, the safety of students from home to school is important. However, it is easier to monitor than students on a bus with one driver who has to watch the road.

WORDS MATTER

Some say that words cannot do harm and should be ignored. However, when words turn into actions that will threaten the safety of students, then they matter. Political correctness has been the target of insults and jokes for years now. Like most generalized statements, this one opens the door to those who choose to define it their way. Some say it tried to keep people from being honest, while others say it stemmed the tide of blatant racism.

Actually, what political correctness accomplished, for good or bad, was to keep bigots in the closet. This was notable after the civil rights movement of the 1960s. For many it made living a little more comfortable, until the dam burst wide open in and around 2016. Hate speech, white supremacy, bigotry, and a wide range of disgraceful rhetoric poured out of the closet into our daily lives under the guise of protecting the people from political correctness.

According to a CNN article on November 30, 2016, nationwide, there have been more than 867 incidents of "hateful harassment" in the first days following the election, the Southern Poverty Law Center says. In a press conference Tuesday, (November 29, 2016) Richard Cohen, the center's president, said he fears those incidents are under reported. This has continued through 2021 and beyond.

The chaos of the influx of this injurious rhetoric was seen by many as atrocious and damaging to the core of society. Others, however, recognize that it is better for those evil thoughts to be out in the open where the perpetrators can be identified, and the words can be countered by those who still believe in some sense of dignity. Now the war of words and ideas continues out in the open where all can see and hear. As they drift into the school, educators grapple with ways to confront it.

The fact that a cross with a hanging noose on it entered into a high school building is the responsibility of the school, and there are no excuses for not responding to it immediately and with the full force allotted the school system. The fact is, however, racist items like this usually come into their building from somewhere else. This is where the family, community, and school system must work together to alleviate the problem. If that can go undetected, what else can?

Whenever something serious is going to happen, someone beside the potential perpetrator knows about it. In 81% of school shootings, someone knew it was going to happen before it happened. Whether the "red flags" come from comments on the internet, or the actions of the individual, if educators have a good rapport with student's they will know immediately to take action. This is not an easy task. It is difficult to read minds, but it is possible to read body language and listen carefully to spoken words to understand the actions of a child in trouble.

Alcoholism, drug abuse, and mental illness go hand in hand. Utilizing the school psychologist, the social worker and a consulting psychiatrist from a local hospital, parents and educators are taught how to look for "red flags" when they show up. Often these "red flags" will be subtle and difficult to discern. The most notable warning signs are when students become isolated. It is the nature of children to belong to a group. If they avoid groups and even friends, they would be worth watching.

Additional signs might include fantasies of violence or acting out violence. This will be difficult to determine as today's video games utilize violence on a regular basis. When observing those acts it would be valuable to see if they were connected to a specific game. If that is problematic, simply ask the student what game they are emulating. If they don't respond, pass that information on to the school psychologist or social worker. In this school the roles of the support team may change.

Psychologists and social workers are often qualified, as therapists, to take caseloads for counseling. It is essential for the school to team with a local hospital that will provide the services of a consulting psychiatrist to meet with an administrator and the therapists on a monthly basis. This will allow for a discussion of students in need as well as general issues facing the school. This is where wrap around services enter the picture to provide support to all. No one can do it by themselves.

SECURING THE BUILDING

In recent years the rise in school shootings has escalated. There are a tremendous amount of guns available to anyone who wants them. Whether bought at gun shops or from a neighbor or a gun show, they still shoot the same. And children still die. Of course, everything should be done to reign in the spread of these weapons. In addition, everything should be done to protect the safety of children in a school building. This building must be a safe haven from harm of any kind. Clearly efforts are being made to protect the children from the coronavirus as it spreads throughout the country.

In addition to the efforts to control the virus, an identical effort must be made to protect the children from the violence which has also spread throughout the country. This, again, is not an easy task but often these two issues go hand in hand. While we assure students are healthy entering the school, we also assure they are not carrying weapons of any kind. This is not limited to urban schools who have been doing this for years, all schools must be alert and scrutinize who enters a building and how they enter it.

A weapon as well as a virus can enter a school unnoticed if we aren't alert. At first thought a prison-like environment might flash through your head. Police in the building, peering in every classroom, a safety aide in uniform, bare walls of prison gray in color, and students marching in lock step from class to class. Not only is this not necessary, it is detrimental to the school environment and thus the students in it. Begin by developing a positive relationship with the local police as a security plan is developed. They must not be a common site in the building but they must be available when you need them.

Here are some common suggestions that come to mind:

- Every possible entrance to the building must be locked or covered by school personnel. Not only does the staff member assure security they also are available to welcome visitors to the school.

- Limited doors must allow easy access for students at the beginning of the day.
- An array of administrators and teachers outside will view the perimeter as well as welcome students. The sooner a potential problem is observed, the sooner action can be taken.
- A check around the doors should assure there are no windows that can be broken to allow access to the door handle, thus allowing access to the school. The best solution are door handle guards as they are hardly noticeable and assure no entrance.
- Strategically located cameras are seldom noticed and do not interfere with the welcoming atmosphere of the building.
- A hotline for neighbors and area business would allow for quick notification of problems in the community.
- A hotline for every classroom would allow teachers to request emergency help while not disturbing other classes. This process could be reversed when all classes need to be quietly informed of an issue.
- A small team of three of four school staff could be made available to quietly respond to a disturbance in the building.

Some of these concerns may sound trivial especially to those in urban schools who have been doing many of them for years. In Sandy Hook the murderer shot through a window next to a door and opened it using the handle. Think of other mass killings in schools in recent history. These thoughts are not trivial. Survey your school and come up with security issues that can be resolved with simple adaptations.

WORKING TOGETHER

Emergency medical staff including the local fire department and hospital will be able to provide services, not only when needed but as teachers in areas of their expertise. Especially valuable is an addition of a permanent school nurse if you don't already have one. There was a time when they were a mainstay in urban schools. Now it is essential for them to be in the building and/or community center for emergencies when needed as well as coordinating a variety of services such as eye tests, hearing tests, vaccinations, and more. The two epidemics of virus and violence must be challenged utilizing every possible effort.

The nurse on sight is helpful as a teacher of many of the health issues in the community. When combining services with the Community Learning Center, a wide range of students and community members could be served. In this day of misinformation, the nurse would be a valuable asset to present the facts to the students. The Community Learning Center, teaming with the school make a powerful team.

The time has finally come to change the way we view schools. Due to the lessons from the coronavirus crisis, the educational world is now aware that, not only are the crisis victims in a dilemma with their skills all over the board, so many Black and Brown students as well as some poor White children have been in the same dilemma for years. Those children, left behind, must no longer be ignored by elite politicians.

This is an exciting, history-making time for those educators who have long wanted a system of education that works for all children not just for the elite. For years teachers have taken the blame for the failings of the current system of education, frustrated by having their voices silenced. Now it is time for teachers to take back their profession, for students to be empowered, and parents to become full partners in the process.

For up-to-date information, visit my website at: www.wholechildreform.com

Bibliography

Allen, William Francis, Charles Pickard Ware and Lucy McKim Garrison. *Slave Songs of the United States,* New York, NY: Dover Publications, 1995.
Beilock, Sian. *Choke,* Simon and Schuster, 2010.
Budzisz, Mary Gale and Eldon "Cap" Lee. *Saving Students from a Shattered System,* Lanham, MD: Rowman & Littlefield, 2010.
Budzisz, Mary Gale and Eldon Lee. *Quashing the Rhetoric of Reform,* Lanham, MD: Rowman & Littlefield, 2005.
Dobard, Raymond G. "The Underground Railroad and the Secret Codes of Antebellum Slave Quilt." *Journal of Blacks in Higher Education*, No. 46 (Winter, 2004–2005), p. 44.
Dye, Dr. Angela. *Empowerment Starts Here,* Lanham, MD: Rowman & Littlefield, 2011.
Dye, Dr. Angela. *The Phenomenon of Powerlessness and Student Achievement,* Minneapolis MN: Capella University, 2014.
Gardner, Dr. Howard. *Frames of Mind,* New York, NY: Basic Books Inc., 1985.
Grandin, Dr. Temple. *Different . . . Not Less,* Houston TX: Future Horizons, 2012.
Gruwell, Erin. *The Freedom Writers Diary,* Long Beach, CA: The Freedom Writers Foundation, 2006.
Harari, Yuval Noah. *21 Lessons for the 21st Century,* New York, NY: Spiegel and Grau, 2018.
Kozol Jonathon. *Ordinary Resurrections,* New York, NY: Crown Publishers, 2000.
Lee, Eldon "Cap." *Brainstorming Common Core,* Lanham, MD: Rowman & Littlefield, 2015.
Lee, Eldon "Cap." *Stop Politically Driven Education,* Lanham, MD: Rowman & Littlefield, 2019.
Lucido, Horace. *Educational Genocide,* Lanham, MD: Rowman & Littlefield, 2010.
Marzano, Robert. *Designing and Teaching Learning Goals and Objectives,* Bloomington, IL: Marzano Research, 2009.
Meier, Deborah. *These Schools Belong to You and Me,* Boston, MA: Beacon Press, 2017.
Ohanian, Susan. *Caught in the Middle,* Portsmouth, NH: Heineman, 2001.

Palsdottir, Hrefna, MS. *"Does Eating Fast Make You Gain More Weight?"* San Francisco, CA, Healthline, https://www.healthline.com/nutrition/eating-fast-causes-weight-gain, June 14, 2019.

Tomlinson, Carol Ann. *The Differentiated Classroom,* Alexandria, VA: Association for Supervision and Development, 1999.

Index

accountability: parent approval, 83–84; school, 82–83, 87–88; student satisfaction, 85; teacher satisfaction, 85, 88–89
achievement, defined, 8, 10, 89–91
Anderson, James, 14
arts, 13, 42–45
assessment, exhibition, 78–80

Beilock, Dr. Sian, 77–78

Cardona, Miguel, 3, 9–10
chaos of change, 98–101, 103–108, 109–111
character development, 45–47
civics, 38–39
community experiences, 26, 51–54, 60–67
community learning centers, 113–115
competition vs. collaboration, 101–102
confirmation bias, 40–42
coronavirus, 1, 31
crisis prevention, 94–96, 120–123
critical thinking, 80–82

diversity, 91–92
Dye, Dr. Angela, 9, 10, 80

empowerment: parents, 25, 117–118; students, 31–33; teachers, 24–26, 102–103, 111–114
expectations, 6, 7
exploratory workshops, 26–28

failure, 22–23, 79
Fitzgerald, Dr. Kara, 4, 76

gap, 97–98
grade levels, 5–7, 23–24
grades, letter, 7
graduation, 29, 86

history of reform, 11

journaling, 47–48

learning, joy of, 12, 13

MAP, 15–18, 19
math, 36, 37

obstacles: childhood stress, 3–5, 76; malnutrition, 3; physical/mental health, 3; sleep deprivation, 3

parent connection, 4–5
portfolio, 18, 19

poverty, role of, 8
project-based learning, 53–54, 56–60

questioning, 39–40

reading clubs, 33–36, 54–56

special education, 19–21

team-building, teachers and students, 67–71
testing vs. assessment, 73–76

university entrance, 17, 18

Weingarten, Randi, 9

About the Author

Eldon "Cap" Lee graduated from Eastern Michigan University in education and received his MA from Cardinal Stritch College in special education. He got his principal's license from the University of Wisconsin, Milwaukee. Since then he has been working tirelessly to bring attention to the failures of the current system of education and replace it with one that serves all children. From his early days as a counselor in a residential treatment center to his years designing the Milwaukee Village School, a middle school in the Milwaukee Public Schools, he has made every effort to put words to actions.

After he realized that his new school would not fit into the current system of education, he began detailing his ideas for systemic change in his writings. Two books co-written with a partner at the school, Mary Gale Budzisz, led to this, his third solo book and fifth book overall. Knowing with every tragedy comes a opportunity, he took a hard look at the coronavirus crisis and saw that opportunity to connect this tragedy with that of the last 200 years. Now is the time for all educators to take a hard look at the system and philosophy of education, and take action!

www.ingramcontent.com/pod-product-compliance
Lightning Source LLC
Chambersburg PA
CBHW030142240426
43672CB00005B/233